The
Superfluous
Anarchist

Michael Wreszin

The Superfluous Anarchist

ALBERT JAY NOCK

BROWN UNIVERSITY PRESS Providence

INTERNATIONAL STANDARD BOOK NUMBER:

0-87057-130-3

LIBRARY OF CONGRESS CATALOG CARD NUMBER: 75-154339

BROWN UNIVERSITY PRESS, PROVIDENCE, RHODE ISLAND 02912

PUBLISHED 1972

PRINTED IN THE UNITED STATES OF AMERICA

BY CONNECTICUT PRINTERS, INCORPORATED

ON WARREN'S OLDE STYLE

BOUND BY STANHOPE BINDERY

DESIGNED BY RICHARD HENDEL

TO SARAH AND DANNY

Contents

Preface

THERE IS renewed interest in the enigmatic and relatively obscure figure of Albert Jay Nock, a latter-day spokesman for an American tradition of anarchist elitism. The term *anarchist*, or *anarchical* or *anarchistic*, is used throughout this study. It is not meant to create an
image of the bushy-haired, wild-eyed, bomb-throwing radical who
stormed the white picket fences of American respectability toward the
end of the nineteenth century—although Nock did ask why in the
world it did not occur to some "enterprising revolutionary simply to
go down to Washington and light a match." Nock has more in common with Dwight Macdonald and Paul Goodman than with Johann
Most and Alexander Berkman. He is closer to what is understood as
American philosophical anarchism—to Lysander Spooner, Stephen
Pearl Andrews, Josiah Warren, and Benjamin Tucker. In this study
anarchism is used in its broadest sense to mean the extreme forms of
individualistic anti-institutionalism described by such historians of
nineteenth-century dissent as Stanley Elkins and George Fredrickson.[1]

But if Nock was an anarchist he was also an elitist. By this I mean
that his anarchist vision rested on the belief that mankind could only
achieve dignity if a select order of superior men were allowed absolute
freedom to think, say, and do what they desired. This peculiar combination of anarchism and elitism is not without precedent in American intellectual history; in America anarchism may well be the most
logical position for the aspiring elitist. Louis Hartz, in his provocative
study *The Liberal Tradition in America*, has described the obstacles
and frustrations facing a man of aristocratic aspiration in the American world of Horatio Alger. For the man who refused to embrace the
prevailing equalitarian ethic, join in the anxiety-ridden quest for
material success, and take on the leadership of popular majorities,
there was little left except the citadel of elitist anarchism.

In his book *The Inner Civil War*, George Fredrickson notes that an intellectual in the period before the war had two alternatives—to embrace the equalitarian ethic or to fight it; intellectuals denounced "not only traditional authoritarian institutions, but also those voluntaristic social and political organizations which denied him recognition. By denouncing the political party and the benevolent society along with the privileged class, the positive state, and the established church, he could call attention to himself as the ultimate embodiment of American individualism." The anarchistic individualism of those earlier rebels became the anarchistic elitism of men like Albert Jay Nock. While this gave the intellectual a sense of distinction in a relatively simple pre-industrial society, it gave him only a sense of superfluousness in the highly centralized, technological society of the twentieth century. Nock's message became Nietzsche's "Where the State ceaseth there beginneth that man who is not superfluous."[2]

It is within this conceptual framework that I have attempted to understand the enigma of Albert Jay Nock. A variety of contradictory labels has been applied to Nock. He has been described as a "radical libertarian"; a "philosopher on the extreme left"; an "old-line right-wing intellectual"; an "unreconstructed Jeffersonian"; a man who, "in spirit, shares that peculiarly American aristocracy that shines forth in the characters of men like Francis Parkman, Henry Thoreau, Ralph Waldo Emerson"; an "anarchist in everything but art"; an "exciting example of conservative political and social thought"; "father of this hardy band" of philosophical anarchists; and finally, a "curious combination of extreme conservative and radical attitudes." I hope that the juxtaposition of anarchism and elitism may clarify some of the confusion and contradiction and perhaps shed light on a rich and enduring American intellectual tradition.[3]

ALBERT JAY NOCK presented me with more difficulties and frustrations than I had anticipated in 1967, when I read a paper on Nock and the anarchist elitist tradition at the Columbia University Seminar in American Civilization (the paper was published in a later form in the summer 1969 *American Quarterly*). In the process of the research and the writing I received help, encouragement, and inspiration from friends, colleagues, and historians. I have attempted to acknowledge my indebtedness in the Notes and Bibliography. I am particularly grateful for the co-operation of Robert M. Crunden, whose valuable study of Nock I have used. He helped sharpen my perspective through a lengthy correspondence and made available to me letters and other material. Miss Ruth Robinson of Wakefield, Rhode Island, graciously talked at length to me before her recent death. Her knowledge of Nock's life and writing was indispensable to my understanding of the man. Lewis Mumford and Geroid T. Robinson provided me with valuable insights and information concerning Nock's career in the twenties. Edmund Opitz and Professor Murray Rothbard, both articulate champions of individualism, challenged some of my views and helped me to see the issues more clearly. Some of those who helped me may be appalled by the judgments I have made and conclusions I have reached. The final responsibility obviously rests entirely with me.

I am indebted to the librarians at Harvard and Yale universities, the New York Public Library, and the Library of Congress. I am particularly grateful to Miss Judith A. Schiff of the Manuscript Division of the Yale University Library and to the staff of the Brown University Library for their efforts in making the work of the researcher as convenient and comfortable as possible. For permission to quote from unpublished material I wish to thank Brooks Colcord, Ralph Hayes, the Harvard College Library, the Yale University Library, and the Manuscript Division of the Library of Congress. The photograph used for the jacket and frontispiece is reproduced through the courtesy of Tristram P. Coffin and Peter R. Coffin. Final preparation of the manuscript would not have been possible without the thoughtful and painstaking work of my editor, Lois Atwood of the Brown University Press. This project was undertaken with the aid of grants from the American Philosophical Society and the City University of New York, and a good deal of the work was completed during periods when I was relieved of my teaching duties at Queens College.

My greatest debt is to Virginia and William McLoughlin, who provided me with lodging and sustenance, both intellectual and corporeal, during summer work at the Brown library. Their capacity to suffer a fool gladly would have rendered Mr. Nock speechless.

The
Superfluous
Anarchist

1. The Anarchist Tradition

ALBERT JAY NOCK is often dismissed as a "neo-Jeffersonian." This unfortunately leads to the rigid and confining conceptual framework of Jeffersonianism versus Hamiltonianism. Every stricture against the state and the centralization of power can no longer be labeled a species of Jeffersonianism. There is an antistate, libertarian tradition in our history that transcends Jeffersonian political philosophy. It is the tradition of individualist anarchism, which was so vigorous in the mid-nineteenth century and which was based either on sectarian dogma or on a significant native radical tradition, that is witnessing a revival in the second half of the twentieth century. If Nock is to be considered a Jeffersonian, then he was an "unterrified" one. Benjamin Tucker, a philosophical anarchist, distinguishing between Jefferson and Thoreau, wrote that "the Anarchists are simply unterrified Jeffersonian Democrats. They believe that 'the best government is that which governs least.'" Then he adds, with Thoreau: "That which governs least is no government at all."[1]

American anarchists drew upon a political and social theory quite distinct from the democratic consciousness of Jefferson, which, in practice as well as in theory, accepted the political process of democracy and demanded the widest possible citizen participation. Individualist anarchism, on the contrary, looked with suspicion on all government as a corrupter of men and a restraint on freedom. Democratic government based on majoritarian principles was no exception. The vision of the individualist anarchists rests on a deep faith in the total sovereignty of the individual conscience. In Emerson and particularly in Thoreau they found far more support for their suspicion of the state and of the inevitable corruption of politics than they could in the thought of Thomas Jefferson, who, despite his eloquent criticism of centralized authority, was a highly political man and an adroit manipulator of power and parties.[2]

The most enduring facet of individualistic anarchism is its extra-political poetic vision. Its advocates spoke for a way of life far more than for a political program or theory. Emma Goldman, who bridged the gap between European anarchism and the American product, put it succinctly when she wrote: "To me anarchism was not a mere theory for a distant future; it was a living influence to free us from inhibitions, internal no less than external, and from the destructive barriers that separate man from man."[3]

A more theoretical and systematic expression of individual anarchist thought may be found in the works of Josiah Warren (1798–1874), Lysander Spooner (1808–87), Stephen Pearl Andrews (1812–86), and Benjamin Tucker (1854–1939). Their emphasis on the possession and use, rather than ownership, of property as indispensable to human freedom separates them from the more communistic and collectivistic varieties of European anarchist thought. Tucker recognized in his theory significant English roots when he described individualist anarchism as "Manchesterism." "For the principle of Manchesterism is liberty, and consistent Manchesterism is consistent adherence to liberty . . . genuine Anarchism is consistent Manchesterism." This explains why individualist anarchists from Tucker and Voltairine De Cleyre to Nock could find such inspiration in Herbert Spencer's critique of the state, and it also illuminates the crossover between the radical humanitarianism of anarchism and some extreme forms of misanthropic conservatism.[4]

Anarchist insistence on the access to natural resources (property) as a natural right, however, hardly supported the capitalist society of nineteenth-century America. The American anarchists conceived of a society of small freeholders and romanticized property as the possession of artisans' tools. Their economic theory was for the most part preindustrial and simplistic. Most of the individual anarchists had little respect for the claims of rugged individualism expressed by the buccaneering entrepreneurs of the Gilded Age. Benjamin Tucker, for example, was critical of Spencer for stressing the evils of government every time it attempted to promote social welfare while ignoring "the far more deadly and deep-seated evils growing out of the innumerable laws creating privilege and sustaining monopoly."[5]

The anarchists of the mid-nineteenth century were persistent critics of the materialism of American life. The acquisition and accumulation of goods beyond the necessities of life appalled them. Like Thoreau they exalted spiritual riches and scorned a society whose main objective was the pursuit of the almighty dollar. They blamed the state for fostering greed, selfishness, and irresponsibility. The anarchist would agree with the conservative critic who charged an excess of democracy, but he would add that there was no excess of liberty. Tucker summoned up the anarchist vision when he announced the publication of his periodical *Liberty*. The magazine's war cry was to be "Down with Authority," and its chief battle was with "the State, that corrupts children; the State, that trammels love; the State, that stifles thought; the State, that monopolizes land; the State, that limits credit; the State, that restricts exchange; the State, that gives idle capital the power of increase, and, through interest, rent, profit, and taxes, robs industrious labor of its products."[6]

Warren, Andrews, and other mid-century anarchists attempted co-operative but individualistic communities as a way of escaping the insidious interference of the state in the private affairs of the individual. These ventures involved the contradiction of simultaneous commitment to co-operative action and insistence on absolute individual sovereignty. They also brought charges of licentiousness, because of the anarchist belief that marriage, an institution created by the state, warped and distorted pure, genuine relations between men and women. Nineteenth-century individualist anarchism combined a belief in libertarian freedom in personal and sexual relations with a pietistic approach to individual responsibility. It was indeed a demanding discipline. As John Humphrey Noyes believed, men "could not become good men by living evil lives, or attain self-government by being governed."[7] Almost inevitably this sincere libertarian faith, with its optimism concerning the nature of man untrammeled by laws and institutions, gave way to bizarre exhibitionism and subsequent disillusionment. By the late nineteenth century the programs of the individualist anarchists were little more than odd curiosities of a less complex time, but the spirit of the anarchist vision endured.

The anarchist faith in the sovereignty of the individual coincided with one of the most cherished myths of the century. The myth of the inexhaustible frontier as a garden of Eden offering men a "gate of escape" from what Thoreau described as "lives of quiet desperation" had an enduring appeal despite its diminishing reality. Individualist anarchism, as the frontier gradually vanished, became more and more a mood than a political or economic doctrine related to specific reform programs. It is the philosophical residue of the earlier nineteenth-century individualist anarchism that has continued to attract some reflective intellectuals who desperately seek an escape from what they consider the tyrannical and controlling mediocrity of a mass society. Henry F. May, in his study of the revolt of the younger intellectuals just before World War I, noted that, for many of them, "Anarchism was at least as much an aesthetic and ethical movement as it was a political program." It regarded democratic politics and the mass society it represented with aristocratic disdain. A kind of elitism entered the language of anarchist rhetoric. Emma Goldman believed with Emerson that "the masses are crude, lame, pernicious in their demands and influence." She rather despairingly concluded that only the "non-conforming determination of intelligent minorities" will ever bring about social and economic well-being.[8]

Max Eastman, whose *Masses* and *Liberator* drew upon the anarchistic libertarian tradition of Emerson, Thoreau, the abolitionists, and Benjamin Tucker, told his young protégé, Joseph Freeman, that "most people today are dead, and therefore those of us who are now alive are doubly precious." From this self-centered assertion it was only a short step to the elitism of Nietzsche, who, Eastman pointed out, advocated the creation of a genuine aristocracy: "And we may as well agree with him, I think, that that is what we want—not a morass of mediocrity, but an eminence, and also a lively dominance through sheer natural force and influence of the people of real ability and value." Emma Goldman documented the assertion: "Nietzsche was not a social theorist but a poet, a rebel and innovator. His aristocracy was neither of birth nor of purse; it was of the spirit. In that respect Nietzsche was an anarchist, and all true anarchists [are] aristocrats."[9]

There is, then, in the American anarchist tradition very often a "simultaneous commitment to the mass of mankind and to a peculiar kind of elitism." There is a strong aristocratic bias in the anarchist politics of antipolitics, which springs naturally from the anarchist's insistence on his individual genius and sense of personal distinction from the rest of society. For these rebels, whose concept of politics embraced a way of life rather than a mundane political program, there was a constant dilemma as to how they could cement authentic relations with the mass of mankind and at the same time stand out against the Philistine, mediocre majority. It is in this context that one must understand a man like Albert Jay Nock as he began his journalistic career on the *American Magazine* in 1910.[10]

ON 7 NOVEMBER 1941 Nock heard from his editor at Harper's, William Harlowe Briggs, who commented on Nock's proposed title for his forthcoming autobiography. It was to be called *Memoirs of a Superfluous Man:* "Ever since you were here I have been chuckling over the title. It is perfect from every point of view, selling books and completely relieving the author of responsibility—either moral or intellectual—you can be as much of an outlaw as you like." The *Memoirs* did prove to be a literary *attentat,* and obviously it was the individualist anarchist capstone to Nock's developing thought over forty years. While working on the final chapter, Nock wrote Paul Palmer, his close friend and former editor on the *American Mercury,* "I am now beginning to throw in the rough stuff." He meant the sustained passages of haughty disdain hurled at the human race and all its works. These were truly the views of a superfluous man who had opted out, was waiting for society to go to hell, and would wish it Godspeed.[11]

Nock's *Memoirs* tells practically nothing about the man. In an earlier essay on the art of biography he had written that one should be able to know a man's mind through his work but nothing *about* him. Privacy became an obsession, and even his closest friends were uninformed about his personal life. They did not know that he had been a clergyman for nearly a decade, that he had been married and had two sons, where he came from, or even where he lived. When Nock worked for the *Nation* he refused to leave a home address at the office. Van Wyck Brooks recalled that during Nock's tenure as editor of the *Freeman* it was rumored about the office that to contact him one must leave a note under a certain rock in Central Park.[12]

Ruth Robinson, a devoted friend of more than thirty years and the illustrator of Nock's *A Journey into Rabelais's France,* believed that he did not deliberately lie about his past; he just did not invite inquiry: "He was not the kind of man you asked questions about. But when he gave himself to a person he gave all of himself. . . . He brought his entire existence with him, but he could quickly depart and when he left he took everything." Nock, late in his life, recorded in an unpublished autobiographical sketch that as a youth he had great difficulty in controlling a violent temper and that as an adult he still was unable to suffer fools gladly. Despite his withdrawn and seemingly arrogant ways he did establish warm and lasting friendships. His colleague on the *American Magazine*, A. A. Boyden, wrote that he "was the sort of a chap that makes a pull on a fellow's affections."[13]

Nevertheless, friendship for Nock was quite obviously a risky affair. After he had attained a modest success as a writer and public figure he frequently wished that he might die anonymously but lamented that the "bitter national resentment against privacy" would prevent such an ending. He flew into a rage and threatened a suit when *Who's Who*, after being denied co-operation, published a fragmentary, inaccurate biographical sketch. Informed that the case was not actionable since he could show no material damage, he wrote bitterly, "Damage to your self-respect and sense of decency doesn't count. That's the U.S.A. for you! Forty years ago I thought I had the lowest possible opinion of this people but it was sky-high beside the one I hold now."[14]

Nock's eccentric concern for the privacy of the individual found support in the anarchist creed. " 'Mind your own business' is its only moral law," wrote Benjamin Tucker, and he took the motto from Josiah Warren. For Nock it was Voltaire's epigram "Il faut cultiver notre jardin."[15]

It is not surprising that so little is known about the first forty years of Nock's life, before he became a professional writer and journalist. His guarded *Memoirs* do not even disclose the place and date of his birth—Scranton, Pennsylvania, in 1870. His father, Joseph Albert Nock, was a clergyman in the Protestant Episcopal Church, and his mother, Emma Sheldon Jay, was a descendant of John Jay. His youth, until early adolescence, was spent in Brooklyn and in Alpena, Michigan. In 1932 Nock wrote with some curiosity about members of his club who seemed to look with nostalgia on their childhood. Nock, on the contrary, claimed to see youth as "something to be got over . . . it has been enormously over-sentimentalized in this country." Romanticization of youth, he charged, was symptomatic of the whole of American civilization, "so deplorably immature."[16]

However, his account of his early years in Brooklyn and Alpena is filled with romantic nostalgia for a time before urbanization, when the pace of life was "kept down to the tempo of the horse-car." Nock's Brooklyn of the 1870s was not very different from his general description of the frontier town of Alpena on the Upper Peninsula. He remembered a quiet suburb made up of sturdy, middle-class citizens with "resources in themselves which enabled them to get on with few mechanical aids to amusement." People were content and even gay. His memories were of a delightfully unrestrained freedom to roam the neighborhood. His friends were well brought up, and for the adults there was no quiet life of desperation. On the contrary, they went about their daily pursuits with good humor and purpose. The cosmopolitan neighborhood—French, English, and German—was tolerant of acceptable nonconformity. Nock presents a stylized portrait of latter-day American purity before the arrival, in the twentieth century, of the "curse of hardness . . . hideousness . . . blighting and dishevelling ennui." This is not the only Brooklyn that the historian knows. At least, it is not that part of the city already in the stages of industrial and commercial transition, with growing immigrant districts marked by "dirt and filth," where "misery, squalor and wretchedness" were the norm. Nock's Brooklyn, like many of his later abstractions, was a personal creation, a kind of barrier serving to justify his vision of the good life. We know from Nock's account what he valued most in that world, but we do not learn a great deal about the actual world that confronted those values.[17]

The theme of unviolated innocence is maintained in his description of Alpena. Through Nock's eyes it seems almost like Brooklyn with rural variations. It apparently had an astonishing number of pleasant eccentrics and general-store philosophers, but above all it was free and independent. All of the human virtues in Alpena flourished in a pure "state of freedom." It was in Nock's again very stylized recollection a community virtually without government. The citizens were "a good lot . . . as far as their lights led them; self-reliant, hard-working, honest, hating restraint, fiercely independent, yet friendly, kindly, and in many unexpected ways, liberal. [They were] standard specimens of . . . the old-fashioned, free-thinking, free-speaking, free-swearing American." Alpena could have served "as a standing advertisement for Mr. Jefferson's notion that the virtues which he regarded as distinctively American thrive best in the absence of government." Nock was certain that the founding fathers would have understood the concept of democracy in Alpena far better than they would "the shoddy article now on sale."[18]

Nock's account of his early education is consistent with the theme of self-reliant individualism. Educated at home under the sympathetic guidance of his father, he found a wealth of material in the family library. Unusually precocious, he could spell out words at the age of three. He remembered that Webster's *Dictionary* was the first book to attract his attention. He may have supplemented it with the precursor of Bartlett's *Quotations,* for he relied heavily on bon mot, quotation, and epigram in all his later writing. "Culture," Nock asserted in the language of Matthew Arnold, who influenced much of his thinking, is "knowledge of the best that has been thought and said in the world," and from an early age he pursued that perfection.[19]

By the time Nock was eight he had begun to read Latin and Greek under the informal tutelage of his father. He was quick to point out that his father never taught him anything but "l'arned" him a great deal. By this he meant that his father took advantage of the raw materials at hand, his son's innate talent and intellectual curiosity (Nock had puzzled out the Greek alphabet by himself before his father took hold), and exploited them intelligently, which was all that education could ever do. There were no schedules, no fixed daily tasks, no regular hours of any sort. Nock studied for the pure joy of it and on his own initiative.[20]

At the age of fourteen he left Alpena to begin his formal education at a small preparatory school in Pekin, Illinois. Again, he remembered a regimen noticeably lacking in restraint. There was no coddling from the masters; each student was expected to find his own way. The school prepared him for the classical collegiate education of the nineteenth century; Nock easily mixed Latin and Greek with an awakening appreciation of German beer and the wholesome "alfalfa-fed" German girls in the community, although very little is said about those extracurricular interests.

After leaving school Nock spent eighteen months reading in a desultory fashion, playing baseball, and working at odd jobs. His parents then sent him to St. Stephen's, now Bard, College, where he continued his studies in the "grand old fortifying classical curriculum." Again the students were strictly on their own—no central meeting place, no encouragement from the authorities, and no discouragement. Nock likened the college to a persevering medieval institution where budding scholars sought out masters and carried on an informal program of "l'arning." This was his understanding of the only proper or even possible way to conduct education. While editor of the *Freeman*, he carried on a discussion with Charles Beard lamenting the demise of such educational procedures, with only the "loosest and most informal organization, with little property, no examinations . . . no ignorant and meddling trustees! A university that would not hold out the slightest inducement to any but those who really wanted to be put in the way of learning something . . . a university that imposed no condition but absolute freedom—freedom of thought, of expression and of discussion!"[21]

It is doubtful if St. Stephen's met this anarchical ideal, which along with Nock's other writings on education is remarkably similar to Paul Goodman's "little treatise in anarchist theory," *The Community of Scholars*, which also laments the demise of the informal medieval scholarly community. St. Stephen's was an Episcopal college, staffed by "stern but distinctive clergymen-professors." How distinguished its training was is subject to dispute. Thayer Addison in his history of the Episcopal church described St. Stephen's, at an undesignated period, as a rather flimsy place. During the very year of Nock's graduation the Society for the Promotion of Religion and Learning gently chided the college for "too easy admissions standards" and urged a stricter marking policy if it wanted to hold the respect of the General Theological Seminary. On the other hand, Richard Gummere, Jr., an admissions officer at Bard College who has looked into this period of its history, reports that the college was a "colorful, rather high quality place."[22]

In any event, St. Stephen's provided Nock with a firm grounding in classical literature and a pride that on graduation he "knew nothing of the natural sciences this side of Aristotle, Theophrastus, Pliny;

nothing of any history since A.D. 1500, not even the history of our own country." A more recent student has supported Nock's recollections of the place by noting with nostalgia that Nock's preceptors at St. Stephen's did not "allow the modern doctrines of equality or democracy on the premises" and that this suited Nock. He was confident that his education had prepared him always to be willing and able, in the words of Plato, "to 'see things as they are.' "[23]

Nock's narrative recalls a sheltered world of individual scholarship and familial bliss—a life totally removed from the boisterous society of the Gilded Age of the late nineteenth century. Occasionally shafts from the tawdry world outside penetrated Nock's smug cocoon. Two incidents of childhood seem to have made a lasting impression, which did much to shape his later attitudes toward politics and custom. The first was a brief encounter at the age of eight with the realities of Brooklyn politics, when that city was ruled by one of the most enduring and flamboyant bosses in American history, Hugh McLaughlin. The boy occasionally watched the activities around the local political headquarters. He observed the drunken rowdies and hangers-on who frequented the place. In the evenings before an election, he recalled that "the Wigwam" looked like "a kind of Malebolge" spewing up columns of drunken loafers who marched around in a frenzy singing patriotic songs. This confirmed for him the popular view that politics was the disgusting vocation of sweating, stinking hoodlums without a shred of decency—absolutely no place for an honest man—a view that he maintained throughout his life.[24]

The second incident, not unrelated, was even more revealing. Nock was only an infant at the time of the Beecher-Tilton imbroglio. But the notorious scandal, challenging so many of the Victorian verities, was a *cause célèbre* of such dimensions that it was naturally a topic of conversation in family circles for years. Nock assured the readers of *Memoirs* that his family did not regard adultery lightly, but "the eye of common sense would see simply that the courts of law, religion and morals were not courts of competent jurisdiction." The courts of taste and manners were; "Whatever law, religion and morals may say or not say, the best reason and spirit of man resents adultery as in execrably bad taste, and from this decision there is no appeal." For Nock, to apply to the courts of law only served to weaken the legitimate sanctions of taste and manners and undermine the development of individual responsibility. Although he failed to mention the Beecher-Tilton affair in the revealing autobiographical sketch "Anarchist's Progress," his attitude is in line with the thinking of the individual anarchists. They insisted on individual responsibility nourished by liberty and free choice and not by coercion, and this is the basis for his ethical code of individual conduct.[25]

Nock's education at home and at preparatory school and St. Stephen's may not have prepared him to distinguish Jefferson's time from his own, but it prepared him for the ministry. He attended Berkeley Divinity School, then in Middletown, Connecticut, in 1895–96 but did not remain to graduate and received no degree. It is believed that he did intermittent graduate work at St. Stephen's, where he taught Latin and German for a brief period. He was subsequently ordained a Protestant Episcopal minister. For a period of nearly twelve years he "stuck it out," as a son recalled, serving as rector of parishes in Titusville, Pennsylvania; Blacksburg, Virginia; and Detroit, Michigan. There is evidence that during this misty past he managed to play a few seasons of semiprofessional baseball, although no record of his incongruous talent has turned up.[26]

These years of Nock's life, from 1892, when he graduated from St. Stephen's, until 1910, when he went to work for the *American Magazine*, are shrouded in secrecy, and only fragmentary information remains. He seldom spoke of them and never wrote about them in any detail. Ruth Robinson, who knew Nock as well as anyone did during most of his adult life, thought that it was the great influence of his mother that caused him, perhaps reluctantly, to follow his father in becoming a clergyman. She noted that he did not ask to be released from his vows until his mother's death in 1924, fifteen years after his active ministry had ended.[27]

Although Nock did not graduate from divinity school, church records make it clear that he became a deacon in 1896 and was ordained a priest in 1897 by William Crosswell Doane, bishop of the Albany diocese. This indicates that his ordination took place in Annandale, New York, while he was doing graduate work and teaching at St. Stephen's. In 1898, shortly after his ordination, he reported to St. James Memorial Church, Titusville, as an assistant to the failing rector, Dr. Purdon. Nock became rector on 1 January 1899, after Dr. Purdon's death.[28]

Nock's elder son, Francis, has recalled a family story of Nock's inauspicious introduction to the town of Titusville. When he alighted from the train, a local sheriff spotted him and immediately hauled him off to the magistrate. A robbery had taken place in a nearby town, and to the sheriff Nock's appearance fit perfectly the description of the thief. Only after a number of indignant parishioners persuaded the officers that Nock was indeed their assistant rector was he released.[29]

Nock had a reputation for telling outrageous stories about himself, and this may be an apocryphal anecdote told to amuse his sons. Nevertheless, it may suggest that from the start he considered himself the wrong man for the job: he apparently never relished the day-to-day duties of a rector. He was not at ease performing baptisms and marriage ceremonies and making the rounds of the congregation. To most, he seemed a loner who spent as much time as possible about his personal affairs or in the solitude of his study.[30]

A brief parish history records that Nock's ministry was characterized by his "brilliant sermons and addresses and by his deep interest in the social order. The congregation was edified by the scope of his learning and his literary attainments." However, others recalled that his display of classical erudition was intimidating to many of his congregation, and the diocesan records show that church membership declined while he was rector. Perhaps in response to criticism, Nock wrote to the vestrymen in 1902 that there was prejudice against the church as existing only for a "select few" and that he was attempting to make it, more than in the past, a church "of the people as it should be." There is no evidence that he was ever able to raise membership, and it is difficult to imagine him as an effective recruiter.[31]

In any event, the church accepted his resignation in 1904, and Nock was called to the rural community of Blacksburg to become rector of the previously inactive Christ Episcopal Church and, for a brief period, chaplain to the students of Virginia Polytechnic Institute, also in Blacksburg. In September 1907 Nock left Blacksburg to take up his last parish, St. Joseph's Church in Detroit. He served there until 15 September 1909, when he resigned from the rectorship.[32]

While at St. Joseph's, Nock published his first article, "The Value to the Clergyman of Training in the Classics." It is consistent with his lifelong championship of classical education, but it also reveals in an unusually formal manner something about his notions then concerning the role of the clergyman and the church in American society. Given his pending departure for reform journalism, it is surprising that the piece is hardly in keeping with the reformist trends of the time. Nock did not disparage concern with social and political affairs but insisted that the church's primary function was with matters of spiritual rather than material progress. The church, for Nock, should be an agent encouraging civilization. By civilization he meant, as he was often to repeat, "the humane life, lived to the highest power by as many persons as possible." He agreed that man's spiritual progress was related to his material well-being, but he argued that religion by its very nature was concerned with "poetic truth" rather than "scientific truth." Religion was "an inward motion, a distinct form of purely spiritual activity." The Christian minister must have for his chief interest "a special mode of spiritual activity . . . interpreting a special mode of poetic truth." Religion should inspire an internal development leading toward human perfection, and clergymen should devote their time to this side of human endeavor. Nock went on to insist that the best training for such work could be found in mastery of the classics. The man who knew Plato and Sophocles by heart also knew "what these great spirits asked of life" and thus to what "their own views and askings had best conform."[33]

It would be unfair to say that Nock believed religion to be nothing more than an intellectual discipline. He often defined it in the words of Matthew Arnold: "Morality touched by emotion." Nevertheless, his superior scholarship and insistence on a rigid classical training probably roused little fervor among his fellow clergymen and parishioners in Titusville, Blacksburg, or even Detroit, which stood on the threshold of its great industrial expansion. Although there is some evidence that Nock met at least one congenial person with whom he could find friendship and share an interest in poetry and literature while in Detroit, his life within the church seems to have been one of lonely isolation. It was too restricting to his deepest feelings about what constituted a humane life. A few years after he had left the ministry and was filled with enthusiasm for his new life, he wrote Ruth

Robinson, asking her what would have become of him had he gone to college and then to theological school and from there to a pulpit: "Wouldn't I have been a daisy? And for that matter wasn't I a daisy five or six years ago? How long it takes to become human under this infernal and devilish perversion of a social system we call civilization." This was written long before Miss Robinson had the slightest inkling that he was, in fact, describing his own experience. The letter reveals the great sense of release he felt after leaving the church. For Nock, organized religion had been encumbered by apparatus and restrictions stifling to the human spirit, which he continued to see at the heart of genuine religiosity.[34]

It is quite certain that he seldom, if ever, told anyone of his clerical past and frequently pleaded ignorance of theological matters. When Miss Robinson had known Nock intimately for many years, she discovered an old photograph of him wearing a clerical collar and asked why he had worn it. He replied that he had once thought it becoming. Referring in the *Memoirs* to his study of Christianity, he noted that it had confirmed his conviction that "the prodigious evils which spot [the church's] record can all be traced to the attempt to organise and institutionalise something which is in its nature incapable of being successfully either organised or institutionalised."[35]

Nock apparently felt the same way about marriage and made scarcely any reference to his own. In 1900 he married Agnes Grumbine of Titusville, daughter of the well-to-do warden of his church. He fathered two sons, Samuel and Francis. He left his wife not long after the birth of his second son in 1905 and is not known to have remarried. He frequently wrote about marriage as a "quasi-industrial partnership" or "business enterprise" but hardly an institution suitable to genuine expressions of love or the natural desire for sexual gratification. He pointed to Rabelais, "who never made a mistake in his interpretations of the spirit of man" and had seen to it that there were no married couples at the Abbey of Thélème. Nock readily conceded that given a regime of restraint, in both custom and law, the majority of men and women would continue to observe the institution of marriage. But he obviously numbered himself among that minority of sensitive free spirits who "see in marriage something which *for them* is unnatural, disabling and retarding."[36]

At one point Nock wrote Ruth Robinson how perfect their relationship was, unencumbered by marriage with its accompanying "devilish sense of obligation. If we had been married . . . and had 'set up housekeeping' as we would have had to do," it would have been a terrible compromise and the giving of hostage to society. Marriage, Nock wrote, would have made him feel meaner because there would be duties that he had to perform rather than a mutual exchange of kindnesses that both felt they wanted to do. As it was, they did these things purely for the sake of their feeling for one another. Thus it would seem that Nock rejected marriage and left the church for the same reasons. He believed both were attempts to organize deep personal and spiritual needs that could be neither organized nor institutionalized.[37]

Nock's references to his personal concerns with women and marriage are extremely guarded, abstractly clinical, and at times defensive. He was attractive to women and enjoyed rewarding relationships with several during his lifetime. Miss Robinson feels that he was greatly dependent on three women in addition to his mother but "interested only in those of exceptional ability and understanding." Later in life his interest in women was platonic, and he was more attracted by their psychical than by their physical qualities, although he did not deny his "connoisseurship" of the latter. He confided to a close friend that he was deeply interested in the duration of man's reproductive power, purely as an index to the duration of general health. He claimed to have been granted long reproductive power, although he had not employed it very much. In the same vague, fragmented sketch he strongly denied having any secrets: "There is nothing in my history that I should have any wish to cover up." In view of the evidence, this is indeed a defensive pose, which suggests that Nock's mysterious personal life included more than a little anxiety and guilt, which were at the root of his obsession with privacy and his sympathetic acceptance of the libertarian, anarchist position.[38]

Nock's profound personal rebellion was an aristocratic revolt, without the flamboyance with which the younger bohemians, who flocked to Chicago and New York after the turn of the century, attacked middle-class standards. But it was similar and, in content, entirely compatible. Freedom was Nock's theme, whether it was freedom from mysterious demons of the mind or from the oppressive restraints of a rigid, smug, and complacent middle-class society. Nock's use of the Rabelaisian image of the Abbey of Thélème is often imitated by anarchist writers. George Woodcock has pointed out that the utopian image of the abbey is the point where the aristocratic and anarchical ideals nearly meet. The aristocrat looks for a society in which there will be freedom for noble men. The anarchist sees one that will recognize the unlimited nobility of free men. The tension between the two ideas worked within Nock throughout his life—leading him to enthusiastic faith in the potential nobility of free men and then to a rigorous defense of more exclusive freedom for a self-appointed remnant of noble men.[39]

2. The Genteel Muckraker

"GOD! it is great to be alive at this time of the world," Nock exclaimed to Ruth Robinson in 1912 after a few years on the staff of the *American Magazine*. "In spite of the misery and inequalities and heartbreaks I would rather live *now* while things are '*doing*' than hereafter when so many of them are all done. If the Lord spares us, you and I are going to have some splendid vigorous years and rejoice in them all."[1]

Nock left family life and the church for the more exhilarating milieu of New York journalism. Although forty years old at the time, he was out to make a place for himself as a writer and social critic. He was working on a novel, attempting to write short stories, which had an almost Jamesian quality, and employed as a journeyman muckraker. He thrived on the bachelor sessions at The Players among such cronies as Ray Stannard Baker, Lincoln Steffens, John Phillips, and John Reed. He was of an older generation than that optimistic group of youthful experimenters who started the renaissance in the years before World War I, but he was caught up in the cult of youth, which saw the possibilities of life as much in a war against the older generation as in progressive politics. "Children of impulse, men and women of restraint, what fools we are, we grown-ups. I wish I could form a compact with some one . . . to obey impulse and live by it for one week, unrestrained, without a single motive an inch below the surface. What a clearing, self-realizing, happy experience it would be."[2]

Nock, to be sure, was interested in politics. But it was politics in Randolph Bourne's sense, a means to life. It embraced a much wider spectrum of human existence than the aspirations contained in the political platforms and programs of the progressives. Reform, for Nock and his associates, was to be a kind of psychic regeneration—achieved not by puritanical restraint but through a rejection of conventional, middle-class morality. He was certain that it was at long last the prophet's age, when the sterile machinery of debilitating politics would give way to a new receptivity to real liberty and freedom: "The people are ready now to hear and learn. They are ready for the best that is in us, and it seems a pity to limit ourselves." Nock's private correspondence reveals that he sought an elitist radicalism that would lead to a genuine democracy.[3]

Bourne expressed similar views. He wrote a friend that "spreading . . . sensitiveness" was "as important as [the work] of the best social reformer." Not until people began to "really *hate* ugliness and poverty and disease" could there be any social advance. Nock echoed this sentiment when he argued that social justice would not be so well served by social workers promoting social legislation as it would by their going "among the unprivileged and teaching them to hate their poverty and misery instead of acquiescing in it; and at the same time, teaching their own friends and families to hate their wealth that has come to them out of privilege, instead of acquiescing in it."[4]

Nock was speaking for the same kind of philosophical anarchism that typifies the radical pietism of such dissenting figures as Fremont Older, Golden Rule Jones, and Brand Whitlock. Nock's introduction to Whitlock's autobiography, *Forty Years of It*, illustrates this kind of moral perfectionism. He described Peter Altgeld and Tom Johnson as "energetic champions of the newer political freedom." He viewed the ethical anarchist Samuel "Golden Rule" Jones, mayor of Toledo, as an "incomparable true democrat, one of the children of light and sons of the Resurrection." Whitlock, Nock wrote, was "one of this noble company," believing with all his heart that the ideal life is practicable. He did not try to bring it on by machinery, by set programs and policies. "He believes in the Kingdom of Heaven as a working fact. . . . He thinks municipal government is not something that can be successfully imposed from without, but that it must express something within. It is an affair of spirit and not of machinery."[5]

Nock was seeking the poet-philosopher-statesman. An admirer of Matthew Arnold, he wanted to find those who could cultivate "that possible Socrates in each man's breast." He was looking for that man who, in Arnold's phrase, had always before him "things true, things elevated, things just, things pure, things amiable, things of good report." A genteel literary scholar in politics, Brand Whitlock, was Nock's American model. By birthright he belonged in the "Eternal realm of divine impossibilities, of sublime . . . inconsistencies." If Nock could believe in Whitlock's ability to apply his ethereal sensibilities to political management on the local level, he was skeptical about his doing so on a national level. He was quick to discourage Whitlock from taking an active part in the new Progressive Party after declining nomination for a fifth term as mayor of Toledo. He reminded Whitlock that Socrates had believed that "in refraining strictly from any direct political activity he and his disciples were the only real politicians of the time." Nock was convinced that the time was "never so ripe for us to keep insisting that platforms and policies are only registrations . . . and to show that *Geist* is the only thing."[6]

This may have been for Nock the only legitimate politics, but it was a politics frankly divorced from power, a politics entangled in the inevitable conflict between the desires for perfect moral order and for perfect moral freedom. It is similar to a radical pietistic strain in America, which defines power and authority as the inevitable corrupter of virtue and the source of all evil. It is a form of nonpolitics, based on innate good feelings, right, and humane thought that slips quickly into the realm of fantasy when it contemplates realization. It is, as Nock understood it, a politics of culture and intelligence—that is, *Geist* as opposed to *Ungeist*—ignorance, irrationality, and narrow thinking. It could be furthered, Nock insisted, not by joining parties or seeking mechanistic remedies but only through "literature, speech and above all, life."[7]

Nock was hopeful that the time had finally come when men like Whitlock, men who believed in the spirit of a nation and in its cultural greatness rather than its accumulation of wealth, would receive popular support. Whitlock as mayor of Toledo had already led the way; his example reminded the "weak and easily discouraged race how high human goodness and perseverance have once been carried and may be carried again."[8]

When Nock spoke of human goodness, as Steffens did of the golden rule, he was not endorsing what he considered the puritanical self-righteousness of many professional reformers. Whitlock wrote that the true reformer was often lacking in humor and mercy: "Without very much of any sort of sweetness and light. . . . he seldom smiles except with the unction that comes with the thought of his own moral superiority. He thinks there is an absolute good and an absolute bad, and hence absolutely good people and absolutely bad people." Bourne spoke with sarcasm of the progressives' "annual contest with the saloon." Nock, with similar exasperation, scorned the comstockery he observed in certain reform circles: "The saloon . . . performs more social service than the churches and organized charities put together." Having only recently made his escape, he was particularly scornful of well-meaning clergymen: "They always want to shut something up—the saloons, theaters, Sunday baseball and so on. My idea is always to open something." Nock had had his fill of ladies who would have the rest of the world moral and proper according to the standard set on Plymouth Rock. Those people who "persistently neglected or violated a natural instinct" were apt to "find it ingrowing into something meaner and dirtier than white slavery." The Puritans had earned the contempt of normal people.[9]

Nock's admiration for Matthew Arnold, the hero of the custodians of culture, may seem curious for a professed radical. But Nock always wanted the best of both worlds. He wanted to be, as he saw Jefferson, a man of radical principles and Tory manners. He was sympathetic to Arnold's attack on the Philistinism of American culture and on the liberals who acquiesced in a life devoted to commercialism. Radicals, he wrote, too often neglected "the social courtesies and minor loyalties of life. . . . We are so taken up with our general love for humanity that we don't have time to be decent to anybody." At this time, however, Arnold's insistence on the bad majority in every society and the need for a superior remnant of disinterested souls to save culture and civilization had little appeal to Nock. He expressed enthusiastic certainty that the mass of men in America were capable of and eager for cultural perfection. The signs were all about him. Chicago, he wrote, had begun to popularize the arts in the best sense. "Really," he wrote, "life here is astonishingly wholesome." The day was not distant when a man could take up a life in politics with no need to compromise and pander. Even marriage, he felt, was on the decline. It would not be more than five years before Americans would have a "lot of cleaner lives and a lot less lying and hypocrisy."[10]

Such utopian hopes as Nock had in the prewar years were destined to frustration and despair, which would lead only to a bitter alienation and the acceptance of some form of elitism. He then held firmly to the anarchist vision of a society sustained by the nobility of free men, but at the root of Arnold's thought, which Nock continued to study, lay the vision of a society led by way of the freedom and authority of noble men.

Ray Stannard Baker wrote of his colleagues on the *American Magazine* that they were men "genuinely absorbed in life, genuinely in earnest in their attitude toward it," not given to dreams of utopias but eager to understand and make sure. Every issue of the magazine, without blueprinting perfection, portrayed a possible, beautiful, wholesome, enriched America, and every writer, even when discussing the most mundane contemporary affair, was dedicated, as Baker put it, to a "happy, struggling, fighting world, in which . . . good people are coming out on top."[11] Nock was no exception. His work ran the gamut from a cheerful, uplifting iconoclasm to a banal form of Horatio Algerism. In nearly every case, whether it was the humanitarian efficiency of the World Scouts or the uplifting lives of successful men, the battle for the Lord was on and victory at hand.

Nock undoubtedly read Henry George during his years as a clergyman. By the time he was on the *American Magazine* he was a devout believer. His work was influenced not only by George's social and political philosophy but by his economic panacea as well. For Nock, George's economics were "fundamental." George understood that man was a land animal and the true doctrine of democracy was therefore public property. By this, Nock understood George to mean that every man had a natural right, if not to ownership, at least to the occupancy and use of land. In 1910 and 1911 Nock wrote a series of nine articles under the general title "The Things That Are Caesar's" dealing with the problems of taxation. They were in the best tradition of the muckraking genre—scholarly, thoroughly documented, naming names, and designed to awaken the public to the iniquities of an antiquated tax system that punished the indigent and aided the privileged class. The antiquated tax policy of New York State with its "inhuman anachronism," the general property tax, and its "unconscionable fleecing of the poor" was little more than a "tax upon ignorance and honesty." This was compared with the enlightened tax on land values levied in western Canada, which was equitable and just. While denying his devotion to the single tax, Nock based the articles on George's economic philosophy; and they held out the utopian hope that George had presented in the latter part of his book *Progress and Poverty*.[12]

The *American Magazine*, Nock wrote, was interested in taxation because it was interested in civilization—"the humane life lived to the highest power by as many persons as possible." Only a fair and decent economic environment could produce a humane society, and the first step must be tax reform: "We want to help create economic circumstances that will take off all immoral pressure from every man, and enable him to be just as good as he might be and as he really wants to be, and would be if he had the power." The abolition of the general property tax and the institution of a tax on land values would, Nock insisted, end the extreme of unearned wealth. It would bring an end to labor agitation. It would reduce idleness, degeneracy, crime, congestion, overstrain, and disease. He was certain that the people would see the light, just as they had accepted the abolition of slavery.[13]

Nock was ambiguous about the role of the state in his discussion of reform. In his appreciation of George's economics he did not then find fault with the implicit confiscation of the rent value of land by the state, which George proposed. Later he saw this to be the one "weak spot in George's social scheme." George knew, Nock wrote, "as well as anyone the monstrously evil character of the American State," and "yet it was to this institution that he proposed to commit the collection" of revenue "from a national confiscation of economic rent, and the administration of this revenue for social purposes." But at this time Nock was concerned with municipal activity, and many anarchists had found George's plan of confiscation legitimate on the community level. In fact, a number of nineteenth century anarchists became enthusiastic single taxers, and others, while opposed to some of George's methods, were fundamentally in agreement with his economic theories.[14]

The anarchist temperament in all times is essentially utopian, and its great strength and contribution lies in its critique of the existing social order. Nock was no exception. He seemed less interested in awakening people to positive collective action through the state than in trying to make individuals aware of the appalling evils of the present system. One of the most perceptive examples of his philosophic muckraking was his devastating attack on the American class structure, in an article on a lynching in Coatesville, Pennsylvania. (It is also an astonishingly acute analysis of the sources of racial violence, written during a period when such analyses were rare indeed.) On 13 August 1911 Zack Walker, a Negro millworker, was lynched by the local citizenry, who believed that he had killed an industrial guard in a fight. Although injured, he was dragged from the hospital still chained to his bed, doused with oil, and thrown on a pile of wood to be burned alive. When he attempted to break away, he was driven back into the flames with pitchforks and fence rails, and the clamorous approval of a crowd numbering in the hundreds. It is reported that the spectators fought over the charred bones and that on the following day children were seen kicking the remains of the torso through the streets of the town.[15]

Nock did not visit Coatesville until a year and a half after the crime, during which time none of the lynchers had been apprehended. The case was still being investigated because of the persistent demands of the National Association for the Advancement of Colored People. Nock approached the case as a detached, scientific journalist attempting to grasp the significance of the crime as a cultural phenomenon and, more important, to discover a rational explanation for the apparent apathy of a society that cared so little to see justice done.

Nock's interest was not in exposing the breakdown of law and order so much as it was in presenting a picture of Coatesville as a typical American industrial community, which, despite its shortcomings, prided itself on having the elements of civilization. The atrocity, Nock insisted, was not one of passion and hate; on the contrary, it revealed the same kind of boredom and aimlessness that prompts street urchins to torture a dog. It was a crime bred of apathy because the life of the average citizen was lived on a plane "where such acts are not seen to be wholly alien, unnatural, and frightful."[16]

Nock did take the occasion to praise the NAACP for its work on the case. He believed that the organization was fighting for a cause that, although unpopular, was essential to civilization—"equality of opportunity for a great, unprivileged, overborne, unhappy section of our people. As long as *any* are victims of inequality, as long as *any* are exploited or dispossessed, there can be no civilization—and this means negro human beings as well as white."

Nock did not feel that the racial issue was fundamental, although he was quick to concede that most Americans considered the Negro inferior and that such things were "a *little more* likely" to happen to Negroes than to whites. But the lynching, as he understood it, was symptomatic of a deeper and more profound ailment that plagued the entire industrial system, which, in the language of Henry George, had "made our immense fortunes and our immense poverty and misery, made our millionaires, made our obstinate inequalities, made our *Hell-holes.*"

He refused to write of the incident with the righteous passion of John Jay Chapman, who had held a memorial prayer meeting in Coatesville a year after the event.[17] Nock's piece, though in parts eloquently moving, was a careful analysis and systematic critique of a social system that inevitably produced "*an upper class materialized, a middle class vulgarized, a lower class brutalized.*" This was the representative class system Nock found in Coatesville—representative because the town was no different from thousands of such industrial towns throughout the country. It was made up of Negroes and immigrants at the bottom, shopkeepers in the middle, and a small resident class of millowners at the top. The smug, close-mouthed complacency of the middle and upper classes measured civilization by the balance of trade, size of population, miles of railway, and number of newspapers, banks, finance companies, and manufactured products. Unless the nation turned away from this kind of yardstick it would fail to produce a civilization capable of progressing toward a "harmonious and general perfection."

In this article, one of the most powerful and prophetic Nock ever wrote, he did not offer any immediate remedies to stop the continued creation of exploitative, industrial "Hell-holes" that bred barbaric, unfeeling citizens. He made it clear that he had little faith in the forces for order. Punishment was useless. Law meant nothing if the people would not back it up. The state, despite its sincerity, was powerless to effect change. An insensitive, brutalized populace would never support law except in its own immediate interest. Only through education would people become conscious of the failings of the American industrial system; only education offered any real hope of amelioration.

Education was the watchword of the progressive era. No other field of reform promised such grand possibilities. Education through muckraking pointed out the evils of society to the present generation. But in education of the child, of the generations to come, there lay the opportunity for social reconstruction. Nock was later to make a reputation as one of the most astringent critics of popular education in America, but in the optimistic years immediately before World War I there were few men in America more enthusiastic about the "new education" advanced by John Dewey and his disciples. Dewey was to write in *Democracy and Education* (1916) that education could be consciously used to eliminate obvious social evils and realize the better hopes of men. Here was a rational, intelligent response to the dangers of industrialization—a way out of industrial "Hell-holes" like Coatesville, Pennsylvania.[18]

Nock's own education hardly offered an example. It was the product of a predemocratic, preindustrial society, which, as Richard Hofstadter has noted, "accepted the leisured and aristocratic view that knowledge is the contemplation of fixed verities." Nock often repeated Matthew Arnold's definition of culture as "knowledge of the best that has been thought and said in the world." In 1914 he wanted to find a way to translate that essentially aristocratic notion into a plan whereby the mass of men could pursue perfection. He firmly believed, along with the pioneers of progressive education, that culture could be "democratized without being vulgarized."[19]

Randolph Bourne is often credited with bringing public attention to the educational ideas of John Dewey and particularly to the Gary, Indiana, school plan administered by William Wirt. Bourne's rhapsodic articles in the *New Republic* in 1915 did create a great deal of attention and discussion. But Nock, a year earlier, had written an equally enthusiastic piece in the *American Magazine*, entitled "An Adventure in Education," which reached a far wider audience. He described Wirt as a revolutionary whose principles could completely revive public education. Nock endorsed Dewey's principle of learning by doing, which he believed was a master stroke of common sense: "We ourselves always learn things better by seeing or doing them than by reading about them." On the other hand Wirt's school was not merely a "vocational" school. He had avoided the pitfalls of offering only "instrumental knowledge." The Gary system would produce skilled plumbers, to be sure, but it would also produce cultured plumbers. Nock was gratified to find that "the literary and artistic side of life" was as soundly developed as its vocational side. Wirt and his colleagues skillfully subjected the students to "the most ingenious and insidious temptations" to become cultured.[20]

It was their method that Nock found so attractive and effective. And, as he understood it, it did not seem remote from his own early training. Wirt understood "that human beings (including children) left wholly free to act and surrounded by free opportunity, will naturally do the right thing as far as they know how." Nock was delighted with the "utter absence of discipline," which was, he wrote, supremely practical "because, being left wholly free in the midst of practically unlimited opportunity, it was [the children's] natural instinct to be good, kindly, and industrious." Like Bourne and Dewey, he believed in the natural development of a child's self-expression. If a child was left free and unfettered he would blossom into a civilized creature with genuine values. The progress of humanity depended on such freedom.

Consistent with Nock's own experience was the fact that the Gary schools did "not try to *teach* anything." They merely offered endless opportunities and imaginative inducements for children to teach themselves. The teachers appeared to have little to do. It was a refreshing departure from the "wearing grind and drive of other schools where the teachers maintain themselves as the center of interest by trying to teach." Wirt, pleased by Nock's sympathetic analysis, wrote a letter to the author, which the magazine published along with the article. He confirmed Nock's insistence that "no teacher can educate the child." Like Nock's father, all a teacher could do was put a child in the way of the materials and exploit his innate imagination and talent.

However, as early as 1914, before the avalanche of criticism began, Nock was aware of the potential perversion of progressive educational theory and practice, which ultimately turned many public school systems into mindless training grounds for "life adjustment" and factories for producing docile and acquiescing citizens.[21] When he went out to

Gary he was full of suspicion and distrust. He had expected to find a "school . . . busily turning out 'useful citizens' in the cant sense, but doing very little for the diffusion of sweetness and light." He conceded that he had been "wholly wrong and prejudiced."

Nock's anarchical temperament made him immune to the distortions of Dewey's principles. Nock wanted, as Walter Lippmann had put it, a life that "shall really be interesting,"[22] but he did not want a public educational system that was no more than a subtle manipulative agency for solving social problems by removing the sources of conflict in life. He always kept before him the anarchist distinction between the *man* and the *citizen*, and he was always afraid that the state would, inevitably, attempt to control education so as to turn the former into the latter. He saw Wirt not as an accomplice to such an insidious design but as a revolutionary, because he saw the Gary plan as an assault on the prevailing system of values. What moved Nock most were not the plan's "mechanical features" but "a spirit, a philosophy, a moving faith behind them," which he compared with the principles of Leo Tolstoy and the anarchist educator Francisco Ferrer Guardia. Now these principles were to be applied on a far more adequate scale. In short, he saw the plan as a way of achieving truly effective popular education, which could subsequently produce a high level of mass culture.

Nock did not identify himself with the poor and exploited in the affected, self-conscious way of many of the more romantic social workers and radicals of his time. Nevertheless, his articles on the Gary plan did not fail to point out its obvious social implications. The success of the plan, he wrote, should put a stop to "our provincial and insular ideas of foreigners—that they won't wash, enjoy illiteracy, practice assassination as a pastime and are radically dishonest." He was certain that their innate but untapped creative energies could be liberated. They too could be participants in a world of sweetness and light if only given the opportunity.

If the progressive era was at times marked by an almost incredible optimism, its enthusiasm reached a peak in the years immediately preceding the outbreak of war in Europe. Walter Lippmann in his book *Drift and Mastery*, which Randolph Bourne "would have given [his] soul to have written," proclaimed victory over the forces of reaction and sterile thinking. The major battles had already been won: "The sanctity of property, the patriarchal family, hereditary caste, the dogma of sin, obedience to authority,—the rock of ages, in brief, has been blasted for us." The new young generation of rebels, he announced, has inherited freedom and a rebel tradition: "The dominant forces in our world are not the sacredness of property, nor the intellectual leadership of the priest; they are not the divinity of the constitution, the glory of industrial push, Victorian sentiment, New England respectability, the Republican party, or John D. Rockefeller. . . . The battle for us . . . does not lie against crusted prejudice, but against the chaos of a new freedom."[23]

It is difficult to discern whether Lippmann's book was a statement of advanced progressivism or an apologia for a new professional business-technician elite. With the downfall of the old conservatism Lippmann announced the arrival of a revolution in business incentives: "The real news about business . . . is that it is being administered by men who are not profiteers." In the same year Louis Brandeis, who was soon to be elevated to the Supreme Court, also discovered that business had become a profession, "an occupation which is pursued largely for others and not merely for one's self." Lippmann was enthusiastic about the development in the universities of business administration schools, which he was certain would take their proper place beside the schools of law, medicine, and engineering. Dismissing the conflicting interests of labor and capital as old-fashioned and irrelevant, Lippmann envisioned a new breed of professionals who had a pride in career and workmanship and were not motivated by the old acquisitive instinct. These new and bold men were at last free from the "higgling of the market." They had developed a "satisfaction [in] services rendered and uses created . . . the civilizing passions [were] given a chance to temper the primal desire to have and to hold and to conquer."[24]

Many of the writers of this period were torn between an awareness of the ugliness, exploitation, and poverty of their civilization and a vision of unlimited possibilities not only in technological development but in the nature of man. Lippmann and others were certain that not only industry but also industrialists would be transformed. Intelligent management would accompany technological efficiency; a humanitarian national purpose would replace the old individual self-interest. Nock was tempted by this fervor. In the Calumet copper fields he saw unbearably feudal conditions, but his letters were filled with new enthusiasm for radical change, which he found everywhere. Labor's rank and file were becoming not only militant but principled. Management was keeping pace. Morgan, he noted, had recently divested himself of twenty-seven directorships. Ford had inaugurated a profit-sharing plan. "It's a big year. How far back in the dark ages all this makes Carnegie seem,—Mark Hanna and the rest, whose word we used to take as law."[25]

Nock's tendency toward anarchic individualism had been a defense against the oppressive power of a privately controlled economic and social system. For a brief period he seemed to compromise his anti-institutionalism. In articles and correspondence he entertained ideas in support of increased state action, but divorced from politics and parties. In August of 1914 he expanded his ideas on the potential of public education and called for an extension of public-school services in which the state would provide facilities for raising infants, to relieve mothers of the burden of child rearing so that they might develop in other directions. This was a reflection of the most avant-garde notions of such feminists as Charlotte Perkins Gilman and Rheta Childe Dorr, who frankly advocated the socialization of child rearing. Nock echoed their arguments when he insisted that the household as an independent economic unit was little more than a nostalgic memory with little relevance to the demands of an increasingly urban, industrial society. Here Nock saw the potential of the state as more than an exploitative political machine. It could contribute to culture and civilization.[26]

At the same time he favored municipal ownership and operation of parks and playgrounds. Cities, he insisted, must meet their obligations. Private charities and gifts blunted a city's sense of its social obligations. They encouraged a system of bribery and corruption that enabled a parasitic class, through privilege and fraud, to live without working and despoil the people of municipal institutions. Nock charged that Carnegie's gifts were vicious in their consequences.[27]

Nock saw change and innovation everywhere and argued that many older social theories needed revision: "Each generation . . . must fix up its own institutions out of the material that the good Lord assigns to it, and not try to fit its life into the frame that was architected by another age. . . . We must do it . . . or fall by the wayside." He was certain that the people wanted a re-examination of their institutions, that they were receptive to substantial change. He believed with Lippmann that the battles had already been won and it was now time to build. He spoke repeatedly of a new understanding of the distinction between the old idea of *government,* which summoned up the principle of partisan self-interest, and the new idea of *administration,* which meant nothing more than disinterested service. It was the difference between the "Tammany idea in cities . . . as compared with the commission or business-manager idea," a popular innovation. Nock was clearly caught up in the movement for managerial efficiency that captured the imagination of so many progressive theorists. But mixed with this optimism concerning enlightened administration was skepticism of the argument that administrative organizations would work for the "national interest." He insisted that no organization or institution should be placed "above the man or the woman." What counted was not what one must do for the institution but what the institution must do for the individual. He felt, it seems, that modern and efficient institutions need not be incompatible with the needs of the individual.[28]

At the time that Nock's writings were most enthusiastic in their predictions for a new order, his interest in the *American Magazine* began to wane; and he was not alone. Lincoln Steffens complained that his articles were being toned down to make the golden rule apply to all but business. Finley Peter Dunne began to break away from the magazine in 1913, and general discontent spread among the older muckrakers on the staff. Nock contributed in part to the decline in quality, by contributing a series of feature articles, on well-known personalities, that conformed to the most banal tenets of success mythology. He was testing the editors' discrimination. He deliberately wrote a piece on Thomas Edison, which he described as the "most insincere, slipshod, exaggerated, meretricious thing that has been written in this city." It was promptly accepted and rushed into galleys. Nock threatened suit if it was published over his name. Its anonymous

appearance confirmed his suspicions that it was time to consider looking for work elsewhere.[29]

Nock did not leave the magazine until 1915, but his interests were
elsewhere and his thoughts "muddled and uncertain." He thought of
striking out as a free-lance journalist, since he was convinced that he
was "reasonably well known to publishers and editors." He considered
going to work full time for some decent politician who was genuinely
interested in economic justice. He had no use for politics or parties,
but he thought he might be able to inject some fundamental principles
into the political arena. He did have administrative and technical
talent. He had organized Brand Whitlock's office as mayor of Toledo
and had served as a tax consultant for local progressive politicians in
Chicago, Baltimore, New York, and New Jersey. He knew and admired Mayor William Jay Gaynor and Governor Martin Glynn of New
York and had personal connections with progressive politicians in
New Jersey. Nock wrote that although he would like very much to
withdraw from the scene and attempt serious fiction and criticism he
did not want to abandon the "fight for economic justice." He wanted
to be remembered as a "good liberal who helped the cause along." He
had nothing but contempt for Roosevelt, whom he considered ambi-
tious and untrustworthy, but after Wilson's election he was receptive
to Whitlock's offer to try and secure him a vice-consulship. Nothing
ever came of Whitlock's proposal, and Nock remained on the *American Magazine* while trying to "take hold" of his life and plan for the
future. On 2 August 1914 he spent a quiet day in New York. He wrote
a few letters from the Café Lafayette and then took an aimless walk
through the deserted Sunday afternoon streets, winding up in Coney
Island.[30]

3. The Journalist as Philosophicker

THE OUTBREAK of World War I was not the trauma for Nock that it was for many. Despite the optimism of his writing in the *American Magazine*, he had made several trips to Europe and was aware of the balance of power that had divided the nations into two warring camps. For a time he was certain that America could remain aloof from the European conflict.

At first he saw the war as a "sad silly performance" not without some compensations: men were slow and weak in learning their lessons, but it should become clear to them just what the system of national governments was capable of. This might awaken them to the necessity of pulling governments down in order to establish rational, intelligent, and disinterested administrations responsive to the people's desires and needs. He saw an awareness developing in the United States, which could set an example for the war-torn nations of Europe when the end came. Americans had shown that they did not accept whatever a government did as legitimate. If the war could bring this lesson of democracy to the peoples of Europe, it would be a "great blessing" and an effective contribution to world peace.[1]

Nock considered himself a pacifist. He opposed the use of compulsory collective force. But he was not rigid, doctrinaire, and evangelical, nor was he inclined toward passive withdrawal from affairs. He felt that the military instinct was a basic human emotion that could be neither ignored nor neglected. He had given the problem considerable thought while traveling in England in 1912 and had come up with ideas remarkably similar to those of William James in his essay "The Moral Equivalent of War."

Nock first wrote about this in an *American Magazine* article describing an organization in England called the World Scouts and led by Sir Francis Vane. He stressed their dedication to humanitarian service as an alternative to militarism. The World Scouts preached and practiced international brotherhood and repudiated nationalistic labels and antiforeign sentiment. They were taught that modern warfare "is neither glorious nor interesting, but, on the contrary, very sordid and stupid." Men did not want to fight one another, Nock continued, unless they were "properly lied to."[2]

The activities of the World Scouts set an example. They attempted to fight the "real dragons," poverty and oppression. He hoped that the movement would spread to America. Reflecting James's arguments and anticipating the ideas behind the Peace Corps, Nock envisioned a million American boys turned loose "to scout the world in search of real chivalrous adventure,—imbued with the idea that the only way to abolish murder is to stop killing people, that the only way to promote friendship is to be friendly." With this kind of spirit let loose, "war would never have a second chance."

As the war raged in Europe Nock continued to believe that the United States not only would remain aloof but would unite in a kind of moral and spiritual regeneration. He was pleased with the attitude of the press; its insistence on neutrality was something to be proud of. Again in the *American Magazine* he asserted that Americans were proving to the world that they were a "thoughtful and serious-minded people. I believe we are forever done with the whoop-la style of patriotism." He saw a new spirit of co-operation among manufacturers, scientists, inventors, and chemists, all devoted to building up the nation rather than to furthering the interests of a privileged class. This was insurance against any move toward war, which was invariably brought about by the interests of the privileged when they gained control of government.[3]

In the December installment of the "Interpreter's House," an *American Magazine* column to which Nock contributed anonymously, he again returned to the theme of his article on the World Scouts. For a "realist" muckraker it is an astonishing example of enthusiastic, utopian thinking. His views now were nearly the same as James's, and he anticipated Randolph Bourne's *New Republic* refinement of the subject in July 1916, "A Moral Equivalent for Universal Military Service." James, Nock, and Bourne were all part of the humanitarian, individualistic tradition. All were suspicious of the state, institutions, and vast organizations. On the other hand, each at one time or another during those years was enamored of the potential effectiveness of organizing and planning toward constructive ends. None denied the absolute need of creating an esprit de corps, a feeling of unity and collective co-operation. James insisted that the martial virtues were, despite their warlike origins, "absolute and permanent human goods." Nock asserted, despite his pacifist inclinations, that the "fighting instinct is one of the noblest we have." Bourne insisted that Americans "craved some kind of national service." The problem was to find a way to channel this basic instinct into constructive energy instead of war.[4]

Nock had seen a hint of such a potential in Vane's World Scouts. Now he saw the possibility of a much vaster scheme that was practicable. In a contrived dialogue between a pacifist philosopher and a poet, Nock, clearly the alter ego of the former, came out for compulsory service for every boy and girl between the ages of seventeen and twenty-one. But the service would be devoted to agriculture, not war. The agricultural establishment of the United States would be designed to take the place of the War and Navy departments. But what of the martial spirit and the fighting instinct? The agricultural establishment would fight—against nature instead of men. Complete with commanders and troops, bands and flags, the organization would be marshalled against floods, grasshoppers, and mosquitos. There would be a standing army of five thousand to do battle at a moment's notice. Nock foresaw a vast army of young people undertaking reclamation projects—"immense areas of dry soil brought under irrigation," reforestation of the entire northwest, reclamation of the lower Mississippi, and power development. It was a vision to make the TVA pale by comparison.[5]

One of Nock's imaginary critics asked where the land would come from to house and train the agricultural army. The immediate answer was, "Confiscate it under military necessity." How confiscate it? At this point Nock brought in his Georgite economics: "Tax it. Exempt all other forms of property and clap every red cent of taxation on land values. Then everyone who held unused land would either use it or dump it, and we would have all the land we need."

Nock, the philosopher, was perfectly serious. His plan tapped the power of innate, aggressive instincts while thwarting the deviousness of leaders who steered people away from their natural enemy, which was nature, and against other men, who were their natural friends and brothers. The establishment of such a program in America, especially while conflict raged in Europe, would make war an American impossibility. Nock insisted that his program combined military training with the "exhilarating sense of real purpose and the still more exhilarating sense of real production, the ennobling and simplifying influence of contact with the soil."

There was in all this a kind of Jeffersonian desire to return to an agrarian society. The agricultural army tied to tax proposals guaranteeing the availability of land to all would create a nation of "real producers, gradually working back to Mr. Jefferson's idea of what we should be." But Nock did not think of it as a return to the past. For him it was to be a national awakening, a great opportunity to undertake a new adventure and set an example for the rest of the world: "A nation full of the fighting spirit, but Hearst-proof and having its spirit intelligently directed against its proper object; a nation of equal opportunity, through the simple device of the landvalue tax; a nation of abounding independence and self-respect; of health, vigor and simplicity; absorbed in the joy of fighting the battles of peace and human welfare;—that is the vision I have of our country, as we have every chance to make it, and should make it."

Intellectual historians of the period have stressed the shock and disillusionment that sapped progressive optimism as the conflict in Europe grew in intensity and the probability of American participation increased. Certainly this reaction can be seen, but it was not the response of all progressive and reform-minded people. To some the war brought exhilaration; it was seen as a great upheaval that would jolt the world out of its complacency and change the course of history. This might not be the intent of the warmakers, but they would not be able to direct the consequences, which could be for progress.

Nock's response reflected this phenomenon. He abandoned much of his anarchical, anti-institutional approach. His own scheme for a gigantic, quasi-military organization for compulsory service hardly seemed a way to reduce the power of the state. But Nock, like other progressive thinkers, saw that organization and administration might lead to a well-planned society, and this briefly undermined his allegiance to individualism.

Even Randolph Bourne, who was soon to recognize war as "the health of the State," echoed Nock's plan for some form of national service: "It could have for its aim the improvement of the quality of our living. Our appalling slovenliness, the ignorance of great masses in city and country as to the elementary technique of daily life—this should be the enemy of the army of youth. I have a picture of a host of eager young missionaries swarming over the land, spreading the health knowledge, the knowledge of domestic science, of gardening, of tastefulness."[6]

William James, Nock, Bourne, and other philosophers of peace were concerned about the quality of American life. To the destructive potential of man, presented in stark relief by the horrible violence of war, they offered an alternative. Nock was certain that a book like that of the German militarist Bernhardi would never find acceptance in America: "When a book is written to prove . . . that humanity's best motive is the sheer lust of power, that love, gentleness and forbearance have no place in the life of nations, that military considerations supersede every other, that the standard man, in short, is a kind of glorified plug-ugly—what are we to say?" Nock insisted that it contravened everything an American knew of human history. It was an aberration of leadership, and Nock was confirmed in his belief that even the German people were not willing followers. It was the state in all its insidious power that had brought about such violence.[7]

At this point Nock attempted to explain the American understanding of individualism and the self-serving doctrine of the superman that had gained such credence in certain quarters in Germany. His language took on a quality almost Whitmanesque as he spoke of the great diversity of American life—diversity and yet unity. Americans were "gregarious and fond of the throng." Nothing, he wrote, was more exhilarating than dashing from the office and hustling "for the Polo Grounds, chinning with Tom, Dick and Harry" and being a part of the "big, good-natured mob that whoops and sweats on the bleachers." It is difficult not to suspect that Nock was writing a parody of the pandering editorials that characterized the *American Magazine* by this time. He wrote privately that it had become part of the "mad passion for size and popularity" and was making him "bilious and out of sorts." Still, one can feel in all of his writing during this period a tension between his insistence on the development of the private self and the deep need for commitment to some transcendent collective endeavor. In this same piece he wrote that America was "a land of big hopes and projects, big dreams and ambitions" and that it had always had a leaning toward the idea of a superman.[8] There is no reason to believe that he was not quite serious. He felt certain that America would someday produce one.

But the American superman that Nock envisioned would not be the egocentric, irresponsible genius of Nietzsche, who seemed "to think the superman's job [was] to hog everything in sight" and felt no need "to justify himself by the ordinary moral codes and conventions that [were] set up for common folks." On the contrary, the American superman would be a "man of sensitivity able to express the collective will, and thus make himself the rallying point for tremendous collective action." It was true that the egocentric superman might build up a *big* nation, but it would not be *great*. The old prejudices—nationalism, diplomacy, secret alliances based on fear, hatred, and cupidity—would no longer work; they thrived on man's meanest passions. There was a job for a new kind of superman, a responsible leader. He could start by uniting the Allies and America in a genuine attempt to liberate "the natural human kindness that is in every soul. . . . Simply taking the lead in making ourselves lovable. That's all. That's the superman's contract, as we see it." The American superman must show the world that the only way to arrive at the good life is by abandoning the petty greed of power politics and embracing some kind of international brotherhood. The first step in a logical program was simply to make America lovable. American leaders should start at home by giving their citizens a square deal. "Love is the master motive of them all. Queer, isn't it," Nock mused, "that all the sovereigns and politicians and diplomats have never found that out."[9]

There is more here than a parody of the banal sentimentality of pacifist rhetoric. Nock had a message for the pacifists that was far more hard-boiled and critical than that of any of the well-meaning writers of peace literature of the day. In May 1915, when the Wilson administration began to embark on a war-preparedness program that disturbed American pacifists, Nock contributed a perceptive article to the *Atlantic Monthly* entitled "Peace the Aristocrat." It was a hard-headed criticism of the smug, liberal pacifism that, in Nock's view, never really got to the root of the problems confronting it. It was superficial and moralistic, based on no awareness of the powerful appeal that war and militarism had for the average man. "Peace the Aristocrat" marks a movement in Nock's political thought away from uneasy association with American liberalism and toward the unique form of philosophical radicalism he adopted in the twenties.

Nock addressed himself to the obvious fact that the man in the street seemed to find war more exciting and alluring than peace. Far from being a criticism of the average intelligence, his argument is of a piece with the critique of American society in his analysis of the Coatesville lynching. Again he saw a society supporting an economic system that materialized, vulgarized, and brutalized its citizens. The average man was immune to the abstract logic of the pacifist and enamored of war and militarism because they appealed to his interest. War, for many, was the great equalizer. It offered an unknown clerk his one great chance in an otherwise "disinherited life." Peace, as it was experienced in America, kept the lower class under the "dragging handicap of artificial distinction and artificial privilege"; war offered a chance of dignity and achievement. War had a second advantage—it appealed to a sense of purpose. It had, to be sure, its perils and horrors, "but the first glad sense of great definite purpose dawning into stagnant and unillumined lives is sufficient to set them at naught." The great "blight of peace is its aimlessness."[10]

In a brief but careful survey Nock described the appalling life of the factory hand who had become so apathetic to the possibilities of life that he passively accepted industrial injury and even death. When peace imposed conditions like these and induced their tacit acceptance, it offered little competition to war. Nock charged pacifist leadership with not understanding the grim alternatives facing the average man. If the United States went to war there would be no dearth of men who could eloquently articulate its high and holy purpose. But who among the pacifists was prepared to express the lofty goals of peace? They could offer no "august and compelling collective purpose" like that available to the war leaders.

The militarists had all the advantages. They exploited the "instinct for responsibility" and tapped the sense of noblesse oblige always "graven on the sword and spear. . . . but never on the ploughshare and pruning-hook." The discipline of war demanded devotion to the common cause, and it punished incompetence and irresponsibility while rewarding service and valor. Did peace, asked Nock, do the same? Did it "degrade the captain of industry who exercises a treasonable oppression? [Did it] cashier the rich man's heir or heiress who does not serve society?" On the contrary, peace rewarded these abuses. War, Nock argued, gave "but very short shrift to such flagrant irresponsibility," which was often the norm of peaceful conditions.

Nock concluded that the common man enlisted in the cause of militarism not "because he loves war, but because he hates peace." It was not without reason that "the aristocratic modes of government always had the instinct to 'keep their people down.' The more drab and unrelieved the conditions of peace, the more gladly will the common man escape them." Nock warned the pacifist that it did very little good to prattle about the horrors of war to a people who are quite "accustomed to actual horrors" of peace. Nock insisted that wealthy and respectable pacifists must take the trouble to transcend their own comfortable but parochial environments and understand that to the disinherited war offers equality; to those forced "to live aimlessly, war offers a clear and moving purpose; and to the finer sensibilities that peace disregards and benumbs, war offers gratification and refreshment."

Through all of this Nock identified himself with those who failed to respond to the logic of the pacifists. "Peace," he wrote, "cannot possibly be interesting or attractive so long as without reason or purpose it keeps so many of us so very poor." He noted with sarcasm that Andrew Carnegie, one of the most famous peace philanthropists, headed an industry that maintained appalling working conditions. In muckraking fashion he recited the despairing statistics of the New York State Factory Investigation Commission to support his charges of hypocrisy and cant. "It is the sheer delirium of vanity to suppose that a peace which permits so many of us to live under such disabling economic circumstances can be attractive, interesting, or permanent. . . . So long as the peace advocates entertain or acquiesce in any such notion, their efforts will appear to us only as the amiable pottering of elderly amateurs."

Nock posed a conflict between the genuine and intelligent aspirations of the masses and the lack of honest insight and imagination of recognized pacifist leaders. These men, he insisted, must come forth as real leaders: "If they will head the gigantic army of Americans who instinctively know how attractive, how interesting and beautiful peace ought to be and might be,—if they will come forward and plan for us and inspire us in order that we can make it so,—we pledge them our confidence, our unfailing support, and our unending patience."

It is clear that Nock believed the mass of men capable of responding with intelligence if that leadership appeared. There is no hint that the potential American superman would be superfluous. On the contrary, Nock believed that the time was ripe and that the people were waiting. The leader need only take up his post.

Nock's critique of the pacifist position was radical in that he called for a fundamental reform of America's social structure. He had not resorted to the traditional clichés of the pacifist pamphleteer but had pointed out the incongruities and failings of existing society. At no other time in his career was he closer to the avant-garde of the progressive movement. His call for mass collective action, his veiled references to intelligent economic reform aided and abetted by the federal government, and his strong belief in the need for responsible, expert, and disinterested leadership were all marks of the progressive theory of men like Herbert Croly, Walter Weyl, and Walter Lippmann. But at the same time his views on the need for collective action were balanced by his innate suspicion of the corrupting action of government: "The thing is, to outgrow governments; the people, left to themselves, don't act that way [i.e., wage war]." Nock wanted leadership that would be no more than a voice for the basically sound, intelligent wisdom of the masses of men.[11]

Perhaps one can read into this grandiose vision of a united people in tune with a creative leadership a preview of the aristocratic elitism that marks the writings of some progressive theorists. But in Nock at this time there was no trace of desire for the kind of mandarin leadership and potential authoritarianism occasionally suggested in the theories of Croly, nor was there the enthusiasm for technological expertise that can be found in Lippmann's *Drift and Mastery*. Nock's views were much closer to those of Weyl, who wrote frequently in the *New Republic* that the masses could spark a reform led by men responsive to the people's needs and desires.[12] Although Nock's ideas are un-tinged by authoritarianism, they are similar to the moralistic mysticism of Edward Bellamy's social theories. His reference to a leader at the head of a "gigantic army" and his call for men who are sensitive to the "collective will" and who will make themselves "the rallying point for tremendous collective action" echo the quasi-military organizational enthusiasm of Bellamy.

Consistent with this utopian perspective is Nock's total neglect of political method and administration. Throughout his essays there is a persistent distrust of the political mind, the institutional approach. Even his call for an agricultural army to fight nature instead of people embodied no organizational theory. A deep ambivalence is always present. On the one hand, Nock warned that the organization must never be placed above the man or the woman: "The great thing is what [the institution] will do" for the individual. On the other hand, there was a desire to belong to a larger, transcendent solidarity. Nock wanted to be a part of the "land of big hopes and projects, big dreams and ambitions." He apparently desired tremendous collective action without government. What he sought was a universal moral upheaval in which the "master motive" was love—a love that transcends nations or continents and "liberates the natural human kindness that is in every soul." This in the spring of 1915 in the face of barbarities in Europe and growing militarism in America hardly characterizes a man of "violated innocence." It is an emotional fervor whose heights of utopianism obviously invited catastrophic disillusionment.[13]

In 1915 Nock traveled in Europe on quasi-official business for Secretary of State William Jennings Bryan. Although the affair is mysterious, it is believed that he was to report to Bryan on the extent to which members of the State Department were co-operating with the propagandistic efforts of the British Foreign Office. Nock, who strongly supported Bryan's adamant position on neutrality, returned abruptly when Bryan resigned from Wilson's cabinet. But he brought home the manuscript for a book written by a former member of Parliament who opposed British war policy, Francis Neilson. Nock arranged for the book's publication by B. W. Huebsch, who was deeply sympathetic to radical criticism of the war.[14]

Entitled *How Diplomats Make War*, it was published anonymously, with an introduction by Nock. Neilson's argument dovetailed the ideas of Nock. He contended that it was governments, not people, that were responsible for war. War was a system of power politics and secret diplomacy; it served concessionaries and political ambition; it was waged for markets and land; and it depended on the "deepening poverty of the lower classes of workers." Neilson was also a confirmed Georgite and believer in what he called "fundamental economics." Nock naturally saw the value of the book in terms of his own ideas. He hoped it would show Americans what the militarists were asking them to support. He was sure that they would be receptive to Neilson's scathing indictment since they were tired of the hypocrisy of conspiratorial "professional statesmen" who lied to the masses; the people were fed up with such deceit, were sick of "sham and sop, of guff and sanctimony; of oily volubility about liberty and humanity." Neilson's book made a splash among pacifist and radical groups in America, and it introduced Nock to the school of revisionism to which he later contributed as the author of *The Myth of a Guilty Nation* and radical editor of the *Freeman* magazine.[15]

During the years immediately preceding America's intervention in the war and up until 1918, Nock was a free-lance journalist. He grew increasingly critical of American society. His firm stand against the war did not endear him to many American publishers. Often his criticism was to be found in pieces on subjects unrelated to the war. Some, nevertheless, offer further expression of his ideas and evidence of his sharpening literary talent. His movement toward anarchism is revealed in two articles on prohibition, which eloquently describe individual oppression by evil government. "Puritanism," perhaps the most popular bête noire of American intellectuals, was the foe, but Nock defined puritanism broadly as a relationship between the state and the citizen similar to that of a guardian and ward; "hence it tends continually toward a more and more intimate and personal regulation of conduct." The puritan believed that "the way to reform society is by putting as many people as possible in jail." Prohibition was the logical application of a "social theory of negation and repression." A society that continued to believe in coercion was incompatible with the good life, the life of culture. The ideals and institutions of Puritanism were "simply unworthy of a free people. . . . Its hatreds, fanaticisms, inaccessibility to ideas; its inflamed and cancerous interest in the personal conduct of others; its hysterical disregard of personal rights; its pure faith in force, and above all, its tyrannical imposition of its own *Kultur*: these characterize and animate a civilization that the general experience of mankind at once condemns as impossible, and as hateful as it is impossible."[16]

Nock was obviously concerned with a good deal more than the aberration of prohibition in Kansas. He was talking about the kind of civilization that could adapt itself to such measures. By 1916 the war spirit was rising in America, demanding increased conformity and reverence for the state. In that year he supported Wilson on the ground that he might prevent American intervention. He wrote Ruth Robinson at one point, "For the first moment in my life I really feel that politics does matter. . . . I think it is really imperative that Mr. Wilson and his present crew, poor as they are, should keep on deck another four years." But his enthusiasm was short-lived. When Wilson decided to intervene it confirmed Nock's belief that no man was immune to the poison of political power: "You can't be a philosophicker and a politicker at the same time." Wilson, he wrote, had tried to "carry water on both shoulders" but had failed miserably. Nock dedicated himself to opposing all aspects of the war effort. In doing so he became increasingly isolated from old friends and journalistic associates.[17]

In July 1917, when Ellery Sedgwick, his editor on the *Atlantic*, supported "sane war-time censorship" of the German-American press, Nock lectured him on the principles of freedom and the obligations of independent editors. They should not allow themselves to become the unwitting tools of the masters of propaganda and deceit. Sedgwick, he claimed, had allowed himself to be manipulated into a "state of sickly dread" when he should be helping to maintain sanity and reason. How can a nation have greatness—"have Geist unless you and I have it?" Nock asked. "It is trying to do without it that has made this mess; and how is the mess helped if you and I let go the little that we have?" A nation's greatness is in its free spirit and not its "armies or censorships or suppressions and commandeerings, and especially not [its] fears." Nock wrote that he had "studied the law of moral action and reaction, whereby hatred gets hatred, and ceaseth not but by love. I had much rather trust myself to the operation of that law than to some little ponderous unhumorous lucubration of a few poor pitiful wretches in Washington, beset and bedevilled as they are by all the demons of need, greed and vain-glory."[18]

What most disturbed him was the apparently easy acquiescence of the liberal intellectual in the demands of the state. Echoing the sentiments of Randolph Bourne, who attacked Dewey and his disciples for their support of the war machine because they had become so enamored of means and had no concept of ends, Nock charged them with pragmatism, with disregarding the "theory of anything." The lack of any overriding philosophy stood in the way of "our being a great people. We are opportunists—in politics, in commerce, in education and in morals." When the war started in Europe, prewar intellectual reformers like Frederic Howe, Lincoln Steffens, and Nock held out the hope that it might serve as a lesson by awakening people to the need of bringing down irresponsible governments—indeed, all governments.[19]

A kind of Tolstoyan anarchism was exactly what Frederic Howe had meant when he described so eloquently a decade later the prewar radicals in his *Confessions of a Reformer*. Filled with guilt and self-depreciation, his *Confessions* documented Bourne's and Nock's charges of betrayal: "I was officially a part of the system . . . I had secret service men in my employ." Agonizing over his role as an immigration official during the war, when he compromised his principles and placed his faith in the state, he recalled, with a sense of relief, his awakening. He decided to speak the truth to fellow intellectuals in the government: "Every one of us had done something to be ashamed of. We have violated our principles, done cruel things." Howe dated his wartime experience as the beginning of real distrust of the state: "It seemed to want to hurt people; it showed no concern for innocence; it aggrandized itself and protected its power by unscrupulous means." The state had not produced the America the reformer Howe had longed for—a nation of self-disciplined, free individuals led by mystical, Tolstoyan anarchists preaching only the wisdom of Christ. On the contrary, it was becoming a land of uninformed pawns, manipulated by managers and masters of deceit. The well-intentioned liberal intellectual with energetic intelligence had become the greatest danger of all.[20]

Nock had warned of this and had refused to succumb to the temptations of the state. He was extremely skeptical of its efficacy in achieving genuine humanitarian goals. He was convinced that it was the duty of the intellectual to remain independent—a "philosophicker" and not a "politicker." As he wrote a friend, "When the good Lord stood us up on the carpet at the end of our course and asked what we had been doing with our talents, we might be sorry we hadn't stuck it out at the old stand as philosophickers."[21]

The prospects of regular work for a philosophical anarchist in wartime were meager. By the fall of 1917 he was determined to write only for the dissenting press, which was rapidly dwindling. It was through the Neilsons that Nock obtained an editorial post on Oswald Garrison Villard's *Nation*. Villard, a staunch pacifist, had taken over the editorship of the magazine and was recruiting a staff of editorial writers who would maintain a critical attitude toward the Wilson administration and its conduct of the war. Nock joined the staff in time to become one of Villard's most articulate critics in the battle against the peace treaty and the League of Nations. His best work was his exposé of the complicity of organized labor with the war machine. At a time when labor might have throttled the state, it was sold out by its opportunistic and unprincipled leaders. Wilson, a consummate politician, had made apparent concessions with great fanfare on irrelevant trade-union issues. But to Nock these were the limited and unimaginative aims of a bread-and-butter unionism that had no fundamental economic philosophy. Labor, he argued, had become absorbed into a system of state control whereby it contributed the sinews of war but gained not a fraction of the profits. It had bartered away its powerful economic weapons when it might have pushed the state to the wall and gained fundamental objectives. Gompers was Nock's special target. His opportunism had cut the labor movement off "from every enlightening and liberalizing influence." In 1914 Nock had enthusiastically seen labor "breaking away from its leaders & taking the bit in its teeth." Gompers had removed organized labor from its tradition of humanitarian, pacifist dissent by expediently spending most of his time in "peevish exhortations to get on with the war." Dissenting labor in Great Britain, however, tried to arrive at underlying principles and refused to be stampeded by the argument of expediency.

European labor, Nock felt, understood that it was not piecemeal trade unionism that leads to genuine democracy but the "diffusion of ownership." It knew that "those who own rule, and rule because they own." American labor, like American liberals, had the foolish notion that the right to vote had something to do with democracy. A labor movement whose exertions helped the aggrandizement of the state was paltry. It was doubly disappointing because it deprived the thinning ranks of dissent of an obvious organization to help in the fight for fundamental economic reform.[22]

Nock was not preaching a war between capital and labor. He was demanding that labor help fight the state, its natural enemy. He really did not develop the Georgite ideas nor give play to the more theoretical economic theories that were soon to engage his attention in the pages of the *Freeman*. These were neglected for the excitement of a new form of polemical journalism that afforded him ample opportunity to display his acid wit and puncture the balloons of the self-important. It also allowed him to remain an independent "philosophicker" while in the thick of the battle.

Nock was outraged when the Wilson administration chose Samuel Gompers to represent American labor at the Inter-allied Conference of Labour and Socialist Parties in London in 1918. Gompers was not respected by European socialists and labor leaders, who were offended by his aggressive chauvinism and denunciation of all radical theory. It was apparent to Nock that the Wilson administration was sending a propagandist rather than someone who would interpret European labor philosophy for American workingmen. It was a deliberate act of state interference and manipulation. Americans needed to understand the conditions and aspirations of European labor, Nock wrote. A well-informed public was essential because the old tripartite division of function in former wars, when an upper class planned and directed, a middle class found the money, and a lower class fought and labored, was no longer possible in any nation. Gompers would return with a report, but it would be little more than a whitewash, diminishing the pacifist inclinations of many of the labor and socialist leaders and expressing his confidence in the unity of working men behind the allies. In a bitter and scathing attack Nock charged that Gompers was nothing more than "a salesman on a drummer's rounds."

The public would get from him at best "the kind of information that a sturdy partisan drummer, travelling continually in an atmosphere of sheer bagmanism, is able to furnish."[23]

Nock's article must have been effective because it caused the Post Office Department to suspend publication of the *Nation*. It is probably the only journal suspended for criticizing a labor leader during wartime, and the suspension supports Nock's charges.

Villard and his editors were spurred on to continue their criticism even after the armistice. Distrustful of Wilson, they wanted a settlement that would not stifle the upheaval taking place in Europe. They wrote glowingly of the "spirit of revolution" abroad that would not die until the peoples of all nations had overthrown "the system" and banished the warmakers. Villard, a mild-mannered liberal, caught the fever. He insisted that only in Moscow had militarism really been crushed to earth. Prussianism still survived in London, Paris, and even America.[24]

This was heady stuff, and Nock threw himself into the forefront of the editorial assault. From the beginning he had opposed Wilson's reluctant decision to participate in the allied intervention in Siberia. Not appeased by official explanations of the need to stop the German capture of strategic materials, Nock wrote that although the President had assured Americans that it was only to be a "very little" intervention it was, in Nock's view, one more example of the enduring system of "secret diplomacy and arrangement." Nock was an enthusiastic supporter of the Russian revolution. He was convinced that the revolutionary leaders distrusted all governments. In the early stages of the revolution he had looked upon the rise of anarchism as the great hope of the world. He remained sympathetic to the Soviet leaders until well into the twenties, certain that they would do away with the political, that is, the exploitative, state and return the land to the people.[25]

During the period of treaty making in Versailles, Nock delivered the most savage attack on Wilson and his policies that had yet appeared in the *Nation*. In Nock's view, Wilson's insistence that the league be an integral part of the peace treaty was a "familiar trick." It was an attempt to dragoon the Congress into accepting a diplomatic conspiracy. It was a league in name only, covering a sinister alliance "of victorious Governments, masquerading under the pretentious lying title," and secretly organized for the purpose of international economic exploitation. Nock tried to make it clear that he did not oppose a genuine league of nations, one that would come when the people threw out the politicians and diplomats and removed economic barriers maintained by "political governments." Beneath the façade of Wilson's glittering rhetoric, however, was the "calm, arrogant, and ruthless formulation of a plan of world-domination."[26]

Nock's views anticipated the general liberal defection that was to come with such mounting fury in the spring of 1919 when Wilson returned to present his treaty and league to the American people. Nock and the editors of the *Nation* carefully exploited the despair and disillusionment, pointing out that they had understood all along the evil design of Wilson and the allied leaders. Intent on exposing the league for what it was and on seeing it repudiated in the United States, Nock's tone became increasingly strident, and his antistatism brought him very close to isolationism. It was time, he insisted, that Americans begin to see that it was futile to meddle in the political affairs of Europeans, who, "if only they were let alone . . . would prove quite able to look after themselves." Nock hoped the politicians would wake up to the obvious fact that "at this juncture a public act of downright, direct, disinterested honesty would turn out to be the most popular" course. Why? Because "popular instinct now . . . is wholly on the side of Richard Cobden's masterly saying, that international peace and good will depend on as little intercourse as possible betwixt *Governments* . . . and as much as possible betwixt *peoples*." Nock was sure that the people, the rank and file, had wisdom and a sense of justice. He only wondered if the politicians and statesmen could run fast enough to keep up.[27]

Nock's common cause with Villard and the *Nation* could not last long. Unity in the interest of dissent was possible, but agreement on a program of reform was another matter. Nock had little more than contempt for Villard's orthodox liberalism. The *Nation's* support of a positive government, which plans for its citizens, and particularly its demands for federal regulation to protect labor organizations were abhorrent to Nock. So was the magazine's timid approval of the socialization of certain industries. They would serve only to strengthen the state. It was beyond Nock's comprehension how Villard could have gone through the experience of the war without learning anything "about the fundamental economics of [the] situation"; the socialization of industry would get nowhere because "economic rent will devour socialized industry just as it devours capitalist industry." In short, Villard's liberalism was incompatible with Nock's single-tax theories and his extreme antistatism.[28]

With the financial help of the Neilsons, Nock resigned from the *Nation* and prepared to publish a new journal. Villard asked him to remain with "the fife and drum of American liberalism." Nock responded that the *Nation* was all that it purported to be—"the foremost exponent of liberalism in the country." But that of course was just the trouble: "I am not a liberal, not in literature, the arts, or public affairs." He assured Villard that his plans to start a new journal would not mean competition for the *Nation*. There were many liberals in the country who would have no use for what he could offer, he was sure. But he was not interested in numbers, just in the authenticity of his wares. With Mrs. Neilson's fortune behind him Nock could afford to be an idealist. Together he and the Neilsons would deal with the fundamental economic questions at the root of all culture and civilization.[29]

For a decade Nock had served his apprenticeship. He had been a muckraking, reform journalist, had traveled abroad, and had engaged in quasi-public affairs. He had commented on daily events and become absorbed in the world of politics and international affairs. He had longed to put out a reflective journal that would eschew programs and politics for critical, fundamental analyses. He felt that he was ready to face the postwar world with a philosophy of life that might not transform society but that would diligently present a standard of morals and manners for well-informed minds. The *Freeman* would be that kind of journal. The venture, he wrote, was "grounded in the belief that the greatest public service" that could be performed at a time when there was a "new spirit of inquiry" abroad was "the promotion of free popular discussion and that a paper which desires disinterestedly to serve its age" would be "interested in discovering popular sentiment," not in creating or manipulating it.[30]

4. The Nobility of the Free Man

By THE TIME the first number of the *Freeman* appeared, on 17 March 1920, Nock and Neilson had managed to recruit a distinguished staff of editors and contributors. On the regular staff was Suzanne La Follette, a philosophical anarchist and distant relative of the Wisconsin senator. Geroid Tanquary Robinson, a young Southerner who lectured on modern European history at Columbia and a former editor of the *Dial,* was scheduled to write editorials and articles on international affairs. B. W. Huebsch was listed on the masthead as president of the *Freeman.* He had published Neilson's *How Diplomats Make War,* staunchly supported avant-garde literature, and been close to a variety of movements for social and political reform. A publisher of Van Wyck Brooks's earlier literary criticism, he persuaded the young man to come to New York to take charge of the literary department.

Brooks and Nock maintained a cordial distance, since in literary matters Nock proved a hidebound traditionalist. In addition Brooks's rather vague, humanitarian, and aesthetic socialism was abhorrent to Nock, whose developing anarchism allowed complete freedom. He looked upon the *Freeman* as a kind of Abbey of Thélème, and the motto for all his staff was "Do what you like." Nock's conception of his role as chief editor was to do nothing. He never gave orders, assigned subjects, or insisted on a general policy. He had only three qualifications for his staff: the writer must have a point of view, he must state it clearly, and he must employ "eighteen-carat, impeccable, idiomatic English." Members of the staff can remember no time when he attempted to revise their work. Copy, including his own, was subject to the managing editor's demands as to space—but that was the only limitation.[1]

In spite of Nock's anarchical approach the paper had a definite policy. Both Nock and Neilson insisted that it be devoid of anything that smacked of latter-day liberalism. When Villard wrote to welcome the *Freeman* into the "ranks of liberal journalism," Nock responded that he hated to seem ungrateful, "but we hain't liberal. We loathes liberalism and loathes it hard. . . . The *Freeman* is a radical paper; its place is in the virgin field, or better, the long neglected and fallow field of American radicalism."[2] In a subsequent issue Nock lectured to liberals on the distinction between a liberal and a radical: a liberal believed the state was a social institution and was dedicated to improving it by political means. Hence a liberal was invariably a slave to politics, programs, and mechanistic reform. A radical knew, not by the a priori reasoning of liberalism but by sound historical analysis, that the state was an antisocial institution, and he advocated "improving it off the face of the earth." Nock was far from applauding the bomb thrower. What he wanted was a sane radicalism; that is, an enlightened economic, rather than political, organization for reform: the state had not been terrorized by Lenin's army but by the impetus he gave to economic organization. Political governments of all varieties, monarchical or republican, existed for one purpose, the maintenance of privilege. The Russian experiment was by original intention and nature an experiment in the abolition of privilege. A purely administrative and nonpolitical government based on economic emancipation would be a threat to every established political government in the world.

The economics of Henry George formed the foundation of Nock's position. Liberals, Nock asserted, mistakenly assumed that there were only two factors in the production of wealth—labor and capital—and spent most of their time seeking an amicable relationship between what they erroneously saw as antagonistic interests. A radical, understanding fundamental economics, recognized a third and decisive factor—natural resources, on which capital and labor were dependent. As long as monopoly interests in natural resources existed, both labor and capital would be exploited. It was monopoly control of natural resources that kept labor and capital warring. A liberal, because of his superficial analysis, looked to the socialization or to the "democratization" of industry as a solution. The radical knew that monopoly values would continue to devour socialized or democratized industry just as such values now devoured what liberals called capitalistic industry. The only solution was to expropriate monopoly interests in natural resources. This was pure Georgite economics, ending always in some form of land taxation.[3]

A vague eclecticism pervaded Nock's weekly editorials and articles, for he had difficulty in applying general theories to specific social and political problems. Lewis Mumford praised the independent and provocative spirit of the magazine: "Obviously, behind these brief generalizations a whole sociology lies, and I can conceive of your performing no better service during the next few years than by slowly building up, clarifying, limiting, and relating the ideas of social development that are therein implied." But Mumford and other readers, who wanted to know just how the *Freeman* stood on specific reforms, were bothered by the magazine's private language.[4]

With repeated allusions to a wide spectrum of sociologists, political scientists, economists, and utopian theorists, Nock's articles were a personal potpourri of diverse ideas and often contradictory theories. Social Darwinism, Manchester economics, and the inevitable land-tax theories of George were combined with other ideas ranging from those of Ludwig Gumplowicz to those of Karl Marx. Francis Neilson, in a character assassination written after Nock's death, charged him with being little more than an intellectual voyeur and a charming but irresponsible confidence man. Neilson's charges were motivated by jealousy over Nock's fame as *the* editor of the *Freeman,* but there was some reason to believe Nock a clever dilettante who weighted his editorial pronouncements by name-dropping. Despite the seemingly fortuitous nature of his grab bag of social theories, a pattern emerges to suggest method in Nock's madness.[5]

If his references to Gumplowicz, Franz Oppenheimer, Theodore Hertzka, and Max Hirsch are not always to be taken as evidence of study in depth, Nock had found arguments in each to support his anarchical distrust of all political institutions. His frequent citing of Gumplowicz is a case in point. There is little to indicate that he had read thoroughly the work of this Polish sociologist who taught for over thirty years at the University of Graz. But even a cursory knowledge of sociological theory at the turn of the century would have enabled Nock to draw upon the group-conflict ideas of Gumplowicz as they pertained to the origins of the state and as they supported Nock's objection to all political authority. But Gumplowicz was an extreme determinist. He attributed no importance at all to the idea of free will and seriously doubted that individuals could in any way shape their own lives or the development of society: "The great error of individualistic psychology is the supposition that man thinks," he wrote. "It is not man himself who thinks but his social community; the source of his thought is in the social medium in which he lives. [Man] is not self-made mentally any more than he is physically."[6]

This is hardly the kind of thought to encourage a budding individualist anarchist. Nor is the deep pessimism that underlay all of Gumplowicz's writing compatible with the perfectionist optimism that at this time characterized Nock's vision. Gumplowicz repeatedly insisted that progress was a meaningless notion, that human intellect did not advance, and that insofar as political and social theory was concerned, men were Stone Age savages and always would be. Gumplowicz conceded that there might be an "insignificant minority" who could perhaps transcend their social milieu, but they were of no importance to him.

If Nock was aware of these pessimistic elitist theories he neglected to discuss them. All he took from Gumplowicz was the idea that the state originated in conquest and confiscation. The futile determinism that was an inextricable part of the theory was ignored. Nock was a philosophical radical, enamored with the power of ideas and the potential of the individual. Gumplowicz's theories on the origins of the state served to destroy its prestige, but Nock was seeking a more constructive theory.

Oppenheimer, who had abandoned the medical profession for economics and sociology, provided the answer. A student of Marx, Proudhon, and Gumplowicz, the German sociologist had achieved a modest international reputation from *Der Staat*, published in 1908 and translated into English in 1915. The book made a lasting impression on Nock, who often employed its phrasing and definitions.[7]

Oppenheimer began with the premise that there were two means by which men satisfied their fundamental needs. One was work, the other, robbery. The first he called economic and the second, political, or the "unrequited appropriation of the work of others." Political means were possible only when all the land had been expropriated. According to Oppenheimer, the historical origin of the state was in conquest, confiscation, and exploitation. On this score he and, subsequently, Nock drew upon Marx's description of colonization, wherein the expropriation of the soil from the mass of the people formed the basis of the "capitalist mode of production." The essence of a free colony, Marx wrote in *Das Kapital*, rested on the fact that the bulk of the soil remained public property available in part to every settler as his private property and individual means of production.[8]

To Oppenheimer the state's record was one of conspiracy and manipulation. Under the control of powerful interests the state denied the mass of men their birthright—free access to natural resources. It is not surprising that Oppenheimer appealed to Nock or that he later became an articulate spokesman for Georgite economics. But Oppenheimer anticipated potential amelioration. He was certain that the system of great landed estates would eventually break down. There was still plenty of free land available in the world, and men would come to see that unhindered access to land was essential to progress. When that occurred the state would lose its power to exploit, and then men would establish a society where only economic means would prevail. In this new society there would be no political structure but only a social structure operating on a system of "pure economics"— the equivalent exchange of commodities for commodities, or of labor for commodities—and the political *form* of the society would be the "freeman's citizenship." There might be an administrative bureaucracy, but it would act only as a guardian "of the common interest," not as the tool of an exploiting class. Oppenheimer envisioned his new society ushering in an "eternal kingdom—from war to peace, from the hostile splitting up of the hordes to the peaceful unity of mankind, from brutality to humanity, from the exploiting State of robbery to the Freeman's Citizenship."[9]

Oppenheimer combined a view of history as conspiracy with faith in the average man's potential ability to break the bondage of the past. Nock accepted not only Oppenheimer's analysis of the exploiting state but also his utopian vision. But it was not quite enough; Nock wanted more color and imagination. He found it in the work of Hertzka, a romancer whose *Freeland: A Social Anticipation*, published in 1891, had competed in Germany and Austria with Edward Bellamy's *Looking Backward*. Hertzka merely transformed the theories of Oppenheimer into a preview of the future. He pictured a utopian society with perfect individual freedom and without any state organization; it would not have judges, police, theft, robbery, or murder. Hertzka actually began a short-lived co-operative community in East Africa in 1893. He attempted to apply communitarian theories that went beyond anything proposed by Henry George, yet Nock repeatedly cited Hertzka's work as an example of a detailed plan of "reconstruction," which—when supplemented by the scholarly underpinning of Gumplowicz, Oppenheimer, and George—met every requirement of reason.[10]

How Nock's eclectic theorizing could be applied to the practical problems of reconstruction facing America in the twenties was not always clear. One reader impatiently quoted a sermon to unions in which Nock had scorned their pragmatic and piecemeal program and had insisted that they should recognize that when the "private monopoly of economic rent [was] done away with," they would not need to bother about such irrelevant questions as wages, hours, and conditions of labor. The reader wanted to know how labor, even if it grasped "the underlying reasons for its state of servitude," was going to change anything if obliged to scorn all political action.[11] What other tangible steps should be taken?

Nock wrote in reply: *"Get wisdom, get understanding."* He pointed out that the editors were not interested in politics or labor reform, thinking it better "to exhibit the economic system upon which the status of labour depends and must depend," regardless of what labor laws might be passed. One did not need to detail a political program: "When people really want something and are quite sure what it is, they have abundant resourcefulness about getting it. . . . When they really want economic freedom and once learn what it consists in, they will not be asking us or anyone else how to get it, for they will be too busy taking effective action on programmes of their own devising." Nock insisted that the *Freeman's* duty was merely to help people understand what economic freedom really was and how, if they acted to achieve it, it would transform their lives even in the "unconsidered realms . . . of art, music and letters."[12]

Occasionally Nock was a good deal more specific. He advocated the general strike as a means of direct economic action: "Grievance before supply," he argued, was an old principle. All labor needed to do was to apply pressure, to walk in on the politicians and threaten that unless demands were met (the end of economic rent, for example) the United States would come to a stop. He made it clear that he did not support trade-union strikes for trade-union ends that merely compromised with a decadent system.[13]

Nock's "anarchism" came increasingly to the fore. Week after week he made flamboyant denunciations of the state and its despotic institutions. He particularly lambasted the law for its alienation from justice. The *Freeman*, he proudly announced, was "never very strong for the Constitution. . . . We sometimes think that it is the appointed function of the United States to clear the way for a regime of philosophical anarchism elsewhere in the world, by its naïve, stolid, unhumorous insistence on showing, in and out of season, what a preposterous thing statutory law is." Kropotkin was now his text: the prince only showed that statutory law was irrational, but reactionaries in America had shown it to be ridiculous. There was nothing like a good crime wave, Nock wrote, to reveal "that 'law and order' is a mere fetich, a creature of rags and wind, and that our reverence for it and our practical dependence on it are egregiously misplaced." People should have contempt for the law because it is contemptible. Instinctive disrespect was, by any objective analysis, justified: "The law is at present probably the most sordid, disreputable and depraving institution in the country"; reason and common sense were above the law.[14]

It was individualist, philosophical anarchism. Despite its apparent call to action, civil disobedience, and even violence, it was ethereal and abstract. The ideas were exciting to Nock and his readers, but they rarely confronted the world of action and commitment. "We are individualists and democrats," Nock proclaimed as he disparaged the efforts of all organizations attempting to achieve any immediate social reform. "We have always objected strongly to the doctrine that man is in any sense his brother's keeper," he wrote while ridiculing efforts at child-labor legislation. Freedom, to Nock, was the only goal worth fighting for: "There is no compromise with freedom. If the principle of freedom be nullified at one point, it may be nullified at any point. . . . Freedom . . . is either a principle, or it is not." Then, in a strangely unsympathetic paragraph on Emma Goldman and Alexander Berkman for their disillusionment with the Russian revolution and their shock at discovering that anarchist radicals were being jailed and murdered, Nock accused them of being doctrinaire. He added the astonishing observation that the "best way to keep one's feet is by trust in the power of the Idea, and by not paying much attention to the ways and means of its development."[15]

It was a strange, uneven performance. Inconsistency and contradiction were combined with frequently penetrating observations on the incongruities of American society. Nock would insist on the need for detached, disinterested discussion while advocating, in inflammatory language, civil disobedience. He would demand adherence to the principles of individual freedom while he apologized for oppression in Russia and suggested that means need not be related to ends. He seldom missed an opportunity to call himself and his associates "radicals —of a theoretical and literary turn." But the claim was supported at best by refined and abstract verbalizing. It was, to be sure, a piquant mixture for members of the Athenaeum and the old abolitionist gentlemen at the Union League Club. But as Lillian Symes and Travers Clement have pointed out, the *Freeman's* rarefied journalism was little more than an "expensive plaything."[16]

Behind all the diverse and detailed economic and political theorizing and the militant calls to action lay a pietistic perfectionism that demanded that word become deed. Nock felt it his job to make the *Freeman* a synthesis of the social sciences and humanities that would be an exposition of the "good life." It was futile, he wrote, to take an interest in achieving social justice unless one really sought a society in which an individual was "free to fulfill the primary law of his being." Why concern oneself with economic fundamentals except as they enable man "to be as good as he knows he ought to be and really wants to be?"[17]

Nock was concerned with the whole life of man, by which he meant culture, and his discussions of economics and sociology were directly related to cultural concerns. The purpose of criticism of the arts—particularly of music and literature—and indeed of all spiritual activities was culture for everyone. Under the present system cultural opportunities were available only to the leisure classes. A responsible critic must always be aware of the relationship of the arts to the economic system under which they are practiced. To be an effective and constructive critic, a man must be enough of an "economist to perceive this relationship and expound upon it accurately."[18]

It is a common but erroneous notion, based largely on Nock's later writings, that during the twenties he was a brother-in-arms with H. L. Mencken, whose astringent barbs on the middle class captured the admiration of a generation appalled by the Philistine quality of American life after World War I. But Nock's bitter *Memoirs* have little in common with the moralistic enthusiasm of his writings in the twenties. He was a severe critic of Mencken's style and approach to social and literary questions. He did not appreciate the "spirit of exasperation" that he judged to be the "feature of Mencken's writing which stands in the way of its getting itself accepted." Mencken's elitist, aristocratic, misanthropic views, especially his skepticism toward the efficacy of ideas, irritated Nock, and on a number of occasions he took the iconoclast to task.[19]

To Nock, Mencken was the perfect example of a critic who had failed to recognize the relation of culture to the economic and political system and therefore had come to the superficial conclusion that culture could survive only under an aristocracy. Nock had no patience with Mencken's glib repudiation of democracy, which he found wanting, vulgar, and degrading because he mistook the American form for real democracy. Nock had no dispute with Mencken's descriptions of mob degradation. But he insisted that this degradation was not a consequence of democracy but of its absence. Mencken used the word *democracy* in a political sense, whereas genuine democracy was an affair of economics rather than politics. The fact that men had votes was no more relevant to democracy than the fact that they had dogs. Nock argued that democracy was based solely on the premise that those who own, rule, and they rule because they own. In a genuine democracy ownership must be diffuse. Votes are useless to people without economic freedom. The form of political government is irrelevant, because government is only the mechanism by which the dominant class exploits the people. The antithesis of democracy is not autocracy but absolutism, which can exist as well in a republic as in a monarchy. What America had been calling a democracy was, in fact, a republic—a republic in which democracy did not exist. If intelligent men continued to confuse this issue, Nock warned, if they conceived of democracy as nothing more than "the right of individual self-assertion in politics," if they made meaningless politics the foundation for their conception of democracy, there was indeed little hope for civilization.[20]

Mencken replied that he had formulated his definition of democracy long ago as "the theory that the booboisie knows what it wants and deserves to get it good and hard." The controversy, despite his facetiousness, was basic. Nock was disturbed not only by Mencken's poor grounding in economics but also by his aristocratic disdain for the average man. Nock believed that the average man could make intelligent political decisions and possessed, at least potentially, discriminating taste. In "The Critic and the Ordinary Man" he came to some astonishing conclusions concerning the taste of the masses in a free society: "The instinct of mankind in the average is always towards the best and if wholly free to choose will always accept and prefer the best." It was a mistake to accept the judgment of pedants who thought that "the taste for the bathos was implanted deep in the soul of mankind." This completely ignored the "perversions, disabilities and degradations" that had "been put upon 'the vulgar taste' by a society which rigorously interdicts freedom to the individual." Nock asked his readers to consider just how much effort was expended by "politicians, war makers, journalists and the like to corrupt and deprave the wholesome average of reason and overcome the average of good sense." In fact, he thought it quite remarkable that popular taste held out as well as it did, considering the enormity of the deliberate subversion it constantly faced. Nock was certain that all the evidence (to which he did not refer) proved that the "average of taste freely developed and freely exercised" showed "an astonishing general agreement with the cultivated taste of the critic." In another context he wrote that the "instincts for freedom, for beauty, for a graceful and amiable social life" were "truly primary instincts" and that all the forces of nature encouraged their development if men were left free and unfettered.[21]

Instead of glibly castigating the masses, Nock said, Mencken might better have devoted his talent and energy to discovering what men were capable of when free to pursue their genuine interests. Perhaps

Mencken was so blind as not to recognize that most men were not free to develop their potential. If this were so, he was an incompetent critic who needed to understand the reality of the society in which he lived and to begin to help "liberate average reason and average taste so that they may function freely and naturally." Only then would he be living up to the obligations of a genuine critic by helping to "transform character" instead of by continuing to pander "for the sake of a kind of delectation" to "vague malevolences, suspicions, repugnances."[22]

What can be made of the aggressive insistence on the potential perfection of man and the excellence of mass culture of this urbane social critic who was soon to quote Henry Adams's dicta that one could never underestimate human intelligence and that nine tenths of the populace were uneducable? Were these statements an elaborate hoax? Or is there within his utopian rhetoric an elitist disdain for the masses he championed? If a saint turns sinner can one find in his early state the origin of his later position? Perhaps Nock's faith was not so much in the potential of the average man as in the efficacy of Nock's own ideas and tastes. That is one definition of idealism—a fervent belief in the power of ideas to transform society. If a man insists that the mass of men can discriminate, analyzing ideas and then acting upon them, and if he then concludes that his judgment is wrong, he can only assume that he, bearing the truth, is apart from the majority of mankind.

On the other hand, Nock's initial position may unconsciously have involved a straw man. Harboring deep resentment and disdain for the unwashed, along with feelings of guilt, he may have so exalted the object of his contempt that it could not possibly have satisfied his perfectionist standards. Then, finding it wanting, he may have established a sufficient rationalization for his own sense of superiority and distinction from the mob. It is significant in this connection that Nock invariably added to his criticism of Mencken's elitism the qualification that if under a free society the average taste proved wayward, the only recourse would be to go over to Mencken and help "rehabilitate the idea of aristocracy."[23]

This speculation, for that is all it is, suggests that Nock's elaborate effusions on human perfectability in an anarchical free environment were little more than a defense for his underlying contempt. Such speculation offers a possible analysis of the change that was to occur in his ideas and a tentative explanation for the more general phenomenon his experience reflects. Biography tends to adapt itself to a catastrophic mode. It relishes dramatic turning points, shocks of recognition, and violated innocence. But perhaps in individuals as in periods of time the seeds of the final stage can be found in the beginning.

Nock's conception of culture, for all his protestation, was from the start elitist and aristocratic. He never transcended his Victorian classical education. Unlike Herbert Read, who as a philosophical anarchist understood that an artisan's work itself could be art, Nock insisted on cultured plumbers. He always conceived of taste and culture as privileged, the personal property of an educated elite—some workers *might* measure up. It was, as he freely admitted, Matthew Arnold's concept of "the best that has been thought and said in the world." This is not only a key to the serious limitations of Nock's aestheticism, but also reveals what he meant by the perfection of taste and reason. It is clear why John Reed characterized Nock as "an anarchist in everything but art." But to Nock art and culture were life.

Not content to challenge Mencken's reputation as a critic, Nock also pointed out the failings of the younger writers whom Mencken championed. In "A Study in Literary Temper" he chided Sinclair Lewis, Floyd Dell, Sherwood Anderson, and Waldo Frank for irritability and lack of sympathy toward their subjects. Because they had axes to grind, their work was distorted; their "master concerns" made them incapable of dealing with universal themes, which could be found among all men. Nock used Gogol's short story "Old Fashioned Farmers" as an example of how vulgar rural material could be fashioned into a story that showed profound concern for the human spirit. Gogol's success, according to Nock, was the result of his love for his spiritual children. The younger American writers failed because they "don't like folks." They were like Mencken, irritable, impatient, and unable to appreciate the potential goodness in all human beings.[24]

Nock did not mean to oppose all criticism of the civilization of "Gradgrind, Chadband and Pecksniff," but thought that their oppressive influence could not prevent the production of good, indeed, classic work, if writers would only develop serenity, detachment, and professional consciousness. They failed in this because they were so absorbed in recording grotesque, tawdry, day-to-day culture that they had neither time nor energy to appreciate and develop great themes. Critics like Mencken were responsible, for they had not tried to make the world's great art and literature attractive and accessible to younger men.[25]

It was a peculiar stance for a self-proclaimed radical who, on the one hand, demanded a transformation of society and, on the other, castigated writers for not remaining aloof from the evils and degradations that plagued society. Again, Lewis Mumford was confused by Nock's ambivalence. He suggested that Nock did not really understand the predicament of the younger literary generation, despite his persistent plea for getting down to fundamentals. Mumford argued that, ironically, it was Nock who was neglecting the "social basis" of the disease that afflicted society. Nock failed to grasp why the new young writers were so restless and so absorbed in daily combat that they neglected their art. It was true, Mumford conceded, that the hero of modern fiction had dwindled in size and that human experience had lost its significance in the din of the "buzzing, screeching, clanking mechanism called modern industrial society." The modern writer was forced to view his subjects as victims of great, overriding forces. To refrain from presenting them as victims, to create out of whole cloth a world of ancient, immutable values in a society where all values were being assaulted, would be to neglect the challenge facing the artist as man. Speaking for the younger writers, Mumford wrote: "We cannot be interested in peoples' lives. . . . We cannot deal with their hopes and dreams and aspirations until they are out of danger. We cannot make friends until we cease to treat victims."[26]

Mumford agreed that a better world would be one in which artists did not have to work under the dictation of master conceptions that turned their material into tracts. Artists should not have to feel an obligation to salvage society. But young writers in America had sacrificed their proper business as artists until society was salvaged. They were caught in a dilemma. They wished to pursue their art, and at the same time hoped to reconstruct their community. They would be unable to devote themselves to artistic work of permanent worth until they had helped bring under control "the strange cyclopean monster

65

that for more than a century has cluttered the world with its Pitts-
burghs and its Glasgows and its Birminghams and Brooklyns . . . and
created the harsh, desolated, spiritually depauperate countryside that
environs them." Mumford was recalling Nock's own earlier imagery
when he had denounced a civilization that gave birth to industrial
hell-holes like Coatesville, but Nock's criticism now seemed aloof and
irrelevant. Mumford wondered what relevance Gogol's story had for
a modern writer. Gogol, he noted, wrote before the industrial revolution had "uttered its birthcry in Russia." But once industrial civilization had begun to scatter its "ash piles and rubbish heaps over the
face of nature," the same tendency to be concerned with the daily
onslaught had captured Russian writers. He reminded Nock that Tolstoy had abandoned his novels to write disquisitions on land and property and that early in this century Artsybashev was complaining
about the "quality of life" in Russia.[27]

There is little evidence that Nock understood Mumford's attempt
to explain the restlessness and rootlessness of younger writers. Apparently missing the point of Mumford's remarks, he said that critics
of his own generation were not doing their duty. Sounding like a
spokesman for the classics-oriented Humanism of Irving Babbitt and
Paul Elmer More, he blamed critics for not keeping interest in the
classics alive by analyzing "examples of great art." He pointed to
Matthew Arnold, Lessing, Herder, Goethe, and Wordsworth as exem-
plary critics. As for Mumford's contention that the industrial revolution had had a serious impact on the artist, Nock dismissed this as
a figment of Mumford's imagination. Hardy and Turgenev had not
been bowled over by the sight of industrial towns because they understood fundamental economics—the old litany, like a Cambridge Platform of fundamental truths. The great writer knew that "the fundamental problem of human society is the same in the remotest village
as it is in Pittsburgh or Birmingham." Mumford's "tearful sociology"
would solve nothing.[28]

Nock always considered a man of "radical principles combined with
Tory manners" the best combination "that human nature was capable
of producing." His literary criticism, its "fundamental economics"
mixed with appreciation of nineteenth-century belles-lettres and devotion to the concept of culture as a kind of depository of great docu-

ments, was a rigid, doctrinaire approach hardly appealing to young writers or radicals. Nock's often didactic tone and haughty display of esoteric and apparently irrelevant allusions served only to incense or bore many of his readers. To Paul Rosenfeld, the sensitive music critic of the *Dial*, Nock was a pretentious egotist who seemed to think he had nothing new to learn. Nock may have read the masters, but it was clear to Rosenfeld that he had understood little and that Brooks, Bourne, and Frank, rather than he, had developed criticism that showed the relationship of every activity of the human spirit to the economic system. Nock, masquerading as a friendly teacher, had demonstrated his complete lack of sympathy for all who were struggling to create a meaningful contemporary literature.[29]

There was some truth in Rosenfeld's acid portrait. In May 1922, when Nock replaced Brooks as book reviewer of the *Freeman*, he was consistently critical of modern works of art, drama, and literature. He wrote enthusiastically of a revival of Sheridan's "The Rivals," but had little to say about any of the newer playwrights. He dismissed free verse as an abortive attempt to rehabilitate prose. He charged that "no sane man" could have written Joyce's *Ulysses*; besides being a dreadful bore it was "pure echolalia" and read "precisely like a stenographic report of the outpourings of excited imbeciles." Although Brooks had reviewed major new works, Nock gave little space or encouragement to anything outside of his conception of good literature, which is really to say that the *Freeman*, despite its erudition, polished prose, and penetrating wit, did little to encourage young writers.[30]

Nock had nevertheless created an impressive monument to his own personality and vision. In spite of the *Freeman's* shortcomings as an organ of critical opinion, it held its own week after week. Nock had, as he often claimed, an almost uncanny ability to "smell out" talent "as quickly and unerringly as a high-bred pointer can smell out a partridge." He was an extremely able editor who inspired the confidence and respect of his associates, and if some of the *Freeman's* readers were dubious about the clarity of its editorial policy, they were quick to praise Nock for its style.[31]

Style and form were important but in the long run were not enough. In the beginning the *Freeman* was unpredictable, provocative, and witty. It engaged the interest of political thinkers of every shade. Georgite theory was still alive among progressive-minded Americans, for its crusading vision if not for its economic ideas. Nock and his associates' weekly criticism of existing institutions and puncturing of pompous balloons were amusing. But always a question remained—where did one go from "fundamental economics"? How could the best that had been thought and said in the world—to many an old, pompous, irrelevant litany—be re-created? Nock might ridicule Harold Stearns's anthology, *Civilization in the United States,* for the lack of depth of its castigation, but he gave little evidence that he understood what prompted young Stearns to write: "We have no heritage or traditions to which to cling except those that have already withered in our hands and turned to dust." And what of social action as opposed to theoretical analysis? The passive radicalism of Nock's utopianism ruled out, as Brooks recalled, one of the major human interests of the time. Nock had stated his rigid theoretical principles and dismissed all specific attempts at social justice as "sentimental sociology." He seemed to abhor piecemeal reform and to prefer passive acquiescence while waiting for the "people" to acquire wisdom and understanding. George Soule, in a survey of the dissenting press in America, wrote sarcastically of the *Freeman's* "exquisite pains" to inform its readers that it was radical. His view of the potency of Nock and Neilson's "fundamental economics" resembled Dos Passos's later characterization of American socialism as being about as "exciting as a bottle of near beer."[32]

There were signs during the last two years of the *Freeman's* four-year existence that the magazine's appeal had begun to wane because of the mechanical predictability of Nock's economic and antipolitical pronouncements. Nock also grew weary of the enterprise, and his faith in the ultimate efficacy of the "leadership of ideas" began to weaken. He stoutly maintained his pose of "radical" democracy's champion, but his exuberance and enthusiasm for the possibilities of a mass-cultured society ebbed. A new tone of resignation, often like Mencken's exasperation, appeared in his articles and editorial comments.

When Alexander Meiklejohn's forced resignation from the presidency of Amherst became known, Nock described him as a misplaced man. He had been unfit for the job—his competence and his genuine interest in education disqualified him for a college presidency in America. This was one of Nock's first suggestions that men of spirit, refinement, and value were superfluous. He insisted that Meiklejohn, as a disinterested independent scholar unhindered by the business bureaucracy of a college, could still perform a contribution by reaching the people directly.[33]

Nock seemed torn between longing for the past and hope for the future. With romantic nostalgia anticipating the more recent idealization of Paul Goodman, he wrote of the qualities of the medieval university, a "community of scholars" where students sought out men of wisdom and there were no examinations, organization, administration, interference from the state, or meddling trustees. His friend Charles Beard disparaged such romanticism as irrelevant to the demands of education in an industrial society. Beard wondered why Nock should lament the passing of universities as centers for genuine scholarship and learning, when one could turn to independent writing, as Beard had done, and reach a far larger audience.[34]

In another context, looking to the future, Nock commented on the career of Charles Steinmetz, a man devoted to science and uninterested in material gain. It would be a hundred years or more, he felt, before the pragmatists, men without principle, compromisers, and worshippers of the immediate and practical would have had their day and Dr. Steinmetz's philosophy of life could be understood.[35]

The past or the future? Nock often seemed to confuse them or to see them as equivalent. But he was increasingly sure that hope for the present was unfounded. He referred to himself as "a veteran of the 'age of innocence.' " He admitted that the "people" were having a better time of it than ever before, but they loved only things. He and his kind were having a worse time. The things the people valued were of no interest to him. Obsessed with motor cars, moving pictures, radios, and cheap popular literature, men were becoming inured to ideas. Interested only in quantity, they had neither conception nor appreciation of quality. The minority—presumably himself and the readers of magazines like the *Freeman*—were "simply out of luck."[36]

Nock welcomed Mencken's *American Mercury* because it would give the "civilized minority" a voice. A subtle hint of nativism began to appear. New Yorkers "of the old type" were becoming rare. Arrivistes attending the opera in white tie, he noted, didn't really look comfortable. He recorded a decline in wholesome American girls in the city and wondered what was becoming of the "good hundred-percent American type." All of this was modified by the ambivalent statement that the "society that has not yet put its aristocracy comfortably to sleep is the society that is farthest from a genuine individualism."[37]

But his optimism about the potential of individuals was diminished by increasing skepticism. Lynching, corruption, conformity, and absurd restrictive legislation were, he wrote, "more or less extemporaneous modes of registering the will of the majority." Quoting Sebastien Chamfort's "How many fools does it take to make a public?" he addressed George Bernard Shaw to suggest that such an acute observer of human asininity come to America, where an incredible wealth of material was available. By 1924 Nock was resigned to the fact that "the Mussolinis [and] Ku Kluxers must have their innings"; the present generation knew nothing of freedom and cared little about it. He had started the *Freeman* on the ground that the time was at hand when ideas would lead, ending the realm of buncombe. Four years later in 1924, he knew that "idealism, i.e., living by faith in the Idea, believing . . . that the ideal life is nothing but the normal life as mankind will some day come to know it," was a risky business. He had learned that it was necessary to take incessant care "to keep one's idealism tempered by shrewdness without letting it be spoiled by cynicism; to keep it sweetened by humour without harshness, and patience without sentimentalism." He no longer wondered "at there being so few idealists."[38]

Nock balanced himself on a tightrope strung between humanitarian faith in the nobility of free men and elitist belief in the freedom of noble men. His last full-length article in the *Freeman* returned to his previous insistence on the potential for wisdom and understanding in all mankind. Almost as if he were lecturing to himself, he charged that only a superficial survey supported pessimism. In a review of the previous decade he admitted that public morals and intelligence seemed to have reached a discouragingly low level. But he called it a natural reaction to the unreasoning passion and emotion exploited by politicians like Wilson. When Wilson's pretentious, deceitful vision collapsed, the people in their impotent resentment had elected Harding and then lapsed into apathy as profound as their earlier enthusiasm. This was a normal phenomenon; the experienced philosophical mind knew that the people would "in time recover and right themselves, as they always do."[39]

Even in the field of private morality the future was not without hope. The people, with their innate sense of reason, would learn the utter futility of trying to legislate morality and responsibility. They would profit by the absurdity of the prohibition laws. He predicted a revival of the "instinctive perception" that most bogus morality, invoked to sanction legal restraints, was factitious and arbitrary. Through these experiences would come sounder understanding and a closer correspondence between genuine morals and intelligence.[40]

In this statement of renewed faith, Nock's earlier confidence was lacking, and his logic and expression were at times obscure. In calling for loyalty to the "Idea," Nock seemed to be responding by rote. He was tired, worn-out, and ill. Returning to his office after an absence of three months, he became more withdrawn and preoccupied. He had not recovered his vigor or enthusiasm, and he was growing estranged from the Neilsons. Neilson remained annoyed by Nock's reputation as editor, and Nock was impatient with and bored by Neilson's stilted, wordy contributions, many of which gathered dust in Nock's desk drawer. Nor did Nock take pleasure in the pedestrian pieces submitted by Mrs. Neilson.

In February 1924, as the magazine approached its fourth anniversary, it was abruptly announced that the *Freeman* would cease publication with the 4 March issue. Nock was already poised for escape and sailed on 11 February for Brussels, which he had described only a few weeks before as "the only really comfortable and congenial place in Europe for a civilized man." It was not long before he was writing friends that he was happy again and that life among the Belgians had renewed his faith in the human race: "What binds me to them is their fierce jealousy, resentment and hatred of all authority. . . . By George, they are the simon-pure natural anarchists of all creation."[41]

5. The Freedom of
Noble Men

In 1871 Henry George noted how "little the people . . . appreciate their true interest" and how easily they were deluded by "words and led by demagogues." Despite his pessimism he vowed to go on, since that was all the "earnest, honest man" could do. Nock, in the mid-twenties, was experiencing the same doubts. During his last months on the *Freeman* his belief in the efficacy of ideas was severely shaken. He wondered how a man could keep his vision tempered by shrewdness but unscarred by cynicism. Editing a magazine, even one like the *Freeman*, was not the way. Raising fundamental questions and applying sound principles to the tawdry, vulgar events of the day seemed to Nock a futile enterprise. Although he, B. W. Huebsch, and the staff stoutly insisted that the magazine had gathered a "fellowship of fine minds in all parts of the globe," Nock privately acknowledged that he could discover little desire for change among more than an inconsiderable minority. But that minority inspired him to go on.[1]

As he sailed for Brussels he decided to abandon critical journalism for scholarship and the study of men of the past who, by their conduct and right reason, set a worthy example for subsequent generations. There was, he found, "a deep curiosity about our history." Scholarship offered an opportunity to "lay a foundation for the benefit of those who come after us . . . when circumstances shall be compelling people to think about changes in their system." Nock was convinced that those who had done the most for the "Cause of Freedom" since Henry George were unconnected with any movement; unconcerned with any program, party, or political policy; and practically unknown as publicists. He chose as examples Frederick Jackson Turner, Charles Beard, and Carl Becker, American progressive historians whose works supported many of his views and who had expressed a deep commitment to individualism and self-government.[2]

For the next fifteen years Nock devoted himself to a highly stylized, impressionistic scholarship that produced unique studies of Jefferson, Rabelais, and George, as well as innumerable articles and essays on the quality of civilization in the United States. In the biographical studies and essays there is always conflict; the alien spirit of right reason always confronted the overwhelming forces of ignorance, conformity, and tyranny.

In an early issue of the *Freeman*, Amos Pinchot noted that "biography is generally autobiographical; and a man's reflections on things other than himself are generally the frankest self-revelations obtainable." Nock's biographical studies support Pinchot's observation. Influenced by the economic interpretations of Beard and the agrarian romanticism of Turner and Parrington, shaped by the theories of George and Oppenheimer, and seasoned with references to Matthew Arnold, they tended to be undiluted studies of Albert Jay Nock, self-professed individualist and philosophical anarchist.[3]

It is not surprising that Nock chose Thomas Jefferson as the subject of his first biography, which was published in 1926, the sesquicentennial year of the Declaration of Independence. Claude Bowers's *Jefferson and Hamilton*, published the year before, had made a great splash, but Nock entertained quite a different objective. His book was not meant to be a popular sensation, he wrote his new benefactors, Mr. and Mrs. Edmund Cadwalader Evans of Philadelphia, nor was it a handbook for vulgar politicians and demagogues. It was to work quietly "and with an effect entirely disproportionate to the amount of fuss made over it." He thought this "the natural way for an influence to work. . . . Experience bears it out."[4]

Nock's *Jefferson* was his first contribution to what subsequently became a gallery of superfluous men. He did not call Jefferson a superfluous man, but his interpretation laid the foundation for a world view that developed into an obsession in the years to come. Even before *Jefferson* he had toyed with the idea. Superfluous men were members of the Remnant. There is something amusing in the fact that Nock chose the enormously popular humorist, Artemus Ward, as a representative man of the Remnant. Ward had appealed to a wide popular audience in the latter half of the nineteenth century, but Nock, in a humorless introduction to Ward's essays, argued that until "the coming of that millennial time when most of our present dreams of human perfectability are realized," the real genius of Ward would appeal only to a select minority. This minority was composed of an order of individuals not associated in any formal way and found among all classes. Its members were distinguished by their *"Intelligenz."* He did not mean the glib and sophisticated as opposed to the obtuse and stupid, or even the educated as distinct from those without education. A member of the Remnant was one who, in Plato's phrase, had the power "to see things as they are, to survey them and one's own relation to them with objective disinterestedness, and to apply one's consciousness to them simply and directly." These fragmented and isolated persons Nock described in the words of Matthew Arnold as the "saving Remnant." It was clear that Nock was not only certain of his membership in the select fraternity, but that he could recognize other members past and present.[5]

Members of the Remnant were outsiders. They were not, he was quick to point out, agitators, revolutionaries, or radical propagandists. They were reflective men who quietly, and for the most part privately, eluded and disregarded "all social pressure which tends to mechanize their processes of observation and thought." Thus they had a critical and indispensable function: to observe things as they really were and record the observations to enlighten their unknown colleagues and posterity. They were the "saving Remnant" because while they constituted only a minute core of *"Intelligenz"* in a vast plain of mediocrity, the seed they cast would take root in some distant future and their numbers would grow, long after they had gone. Ward, Jefferson, Rabelais, and George were all members of this noble order. They were part of a great tradition that would be recognized when men were forced to return to the humane life or face the catastrophe of complete disintegration. For Nock, the future now lay with the Remnant, to whose members he addressed himself.[6]

Nock's impressionistic analysis of Jefferson is a detailed study of a man who, despite his public career, really only spoke to and for the Remnant. His enduring contribution was not to be found in his public role as a politician or statesman, any more than Ward's significance lay in his popular reputation as a humorist, or Henry George's in his as a reformer. These aspects of their careers were public property, but their true importance lay in their minds—in their intellectual activity and sensitivity. Nock, who ignored or passed over briefly the usual details of his subject's life, had a special purpose—to present "a study in conduct and character," to discover and present Jefferson's philosophy of existence. He did not deny the importance of Jefferson's participation in affairs of state, but Nock was more interested in what lay behind that participation. It was certain, Nock later wrote, "that whatever a man may do or say, the most significant thing about him is what he thinks . . . how he came to think it, why he continued to think it, or . . . what the influences were which caused him to change his mind." Nock's *Jefferson*, drawn so much from its author's personal, introspective judgments, constituted, in its way, the first volume of his "autobiography of a mind," the *Memoirs of a Superfluous Man.*[7]

Through Nock's lenses a different Jefferson emerges. He conforms in nearly every particular to Nock's vision of a select member of the saving Remnant. Nock first pictures Jefferson as the youngest of a learned coterie that included Dr. William Small, George Wythe, and Francis Fauquier—men of philosophic tastes and refinement, intellectual curiosity and discrimination, "alien spirits" in the cultural backwater of Williamsburg, Virginia, who had been quick to recognize in Jefferson one of themselves. He appears, from the start, as an outsider representing an exclusive society of New World philosophes. Nock was entranced by an early letter in which Jefferson proposed a secret language "which shall be totally unintelligible to every one" but the writer and his correspondent.[8]

In a remarkable piece of self-characterization Nock described a secretive Jefferson living up to Epicurus's dictum *"Hide thy life."* Jefferson, Nock records, was a master "at hiding his inner springs of sentiment." He was "the most approachable and the most impenetrable of men, easy and delightful of acquaintance, impossible of knowledge." In a charming description of Jefferson in the salon of Mme de Staël, Nock portrayed his subject moving "with the high step and arched back of feline circumspection." This pen portrait conforms in the memory of Nock's friends to his own aloof, aristocratic bearing. As the historian Richard Hofstadter has claimed, Nock knew his subject, perhaps because he created a Jefferson with the inner vision, aspiration, and values of Albert Jay Nock. But it should also be understood that Nock's interpretation of Jefferson was a good deal more provocative and penetrating than some of the orthodox versions produced by rigid, unimaginative liberal mythology.[9]

By Nock's tally, Jefferson's opinions, tastes, and judgments conformed to his own. Jefferson, he felt, also really understood how far removed legal theory and practice were from justice. Jefferson, as well, distrusted politicians and politics, for which he had, according to Nock, neither skill nor inclination; he lacked the "peculiar gifts of persuasion and bargaining" necessary for the pandering of politics. Nock was sure that even before he became governor, diplomat, and president, Jefferson had lost interest in public affairs; without worldly ambition, distrustful of power, Jefferson had reluctantly served the public from a sense of obligation. His experience as governor of Virginia hardly afforded him satisfaction or pride, since he was constantly "at the mercy of a crew of third-rate people" and had to expose himself to "the brunt of ignorance, slackness, stupidity, irresponsibility and petty self-interest."[10]

As a member of Washington's cabinet, as vice-president, and as president, Nock's hero and alter ego always remained above "the dishevelling squalor of routine politics." Driven by a singleminded, disinterested vision of justice and integrity, the Jefferson whom Nock knew never stooped to petty political dealing. Jefferson, he wrote, had a positive distaste for controversy and was thus "a poor disputant . . . finding in [contention] a touch of vulgarity." In his political feuds with Marshall and Hamilton, Jefferson never "permitted himself to bear [the] mark of immaturity" of letting opinions "act as a divisive force between individuals." He always treated opponents with respect and dignity. Indeed, this saintly portrait reaches an apex with Nock's insistence that it was difficult for Jefferson to be "strictly just" in his suspicion of Aaron Burr but his distrust "never degenerated into anything like personal enmity."[11]

Nock's Jefferson is a loser in politics. He fails in his battles with Hamilton, Marshall, and Burr, but in these failures Nock finds his greatness. Jefferson was "a man for whom conduct was three-fourths of life and good taste nine-tenths of conduct," and these, Nock judged, were hardly qualities that fitted him for a politician's role. Jefferson had gravitated through circumstance and a sense of duty "into the position, quite alien to his natural bent, of leadership in a great popular movement"; Nock was sure that Jefferson had never been the philosopher or strategist of a partisan political movement. He portrays Jefferson as a reluctant victim who responded only with misgivings, relieved when he was able to return to scholarship and speculation at Monticello.[12]

The other Jefferson—equally familiar to historians—a man of acute political wisdom, creator of a party and well-oiled machine, who distrusted power but seldom misunderstood its uses, was not entirely neglected by Nock. But here his interpretation is routine, taken, as Nock readily admitted, from Charles Beard's work on the economic origins of the Constitution and Jeffersonian democracy. With this as a framework Nock explains Jefferson's weakness; he had an uncertain grasp of "fundamental economics." He had, to be sure, "occasional brilliant flashes of insight" and, at times, recognized the relationship between government and economics, but such "flashes" were "too brief and unsteady to be illuminating." Jefferson, Nock felt, understood the essential concept that "the earth is given as a common stock for man to labour and live on." He also seemed to recognize that the "natural progress of things is for liberty to yield and government to gain ground." His instinctive distrust of parties and politics was sound, and therefore, even without a firm grasp of the economic issues, he was on the side of the angels. But in his dispute with Hamilton he was never able to put things together in such a way as really to see the insidious aspects of Hamilton's program.[13]

In Nock's view, neither Jefferson nor Hamilton was able to penetrate beneath his own political rhetoric. Jefferson, missing the economic objectives of Hamilton's system, railed at his apparent penchant for monarchy and his Anglomania. Hamilton, confused by Jefferson's stubborn intransigence, attributed it to his "womanish attachment to France and . . . resentment against Great Britain." In the heat of the struggle, Nock argued, neither saw the obvious. Both turned the debate into distorted politics and ideology when the issues were simply economic. Jefferson was no more of a theoretical democrat than Hamilton, said Nock, but was merely for "control of government by the producing class." Adopting the nomenclature of Oppenheimer, Nock saw Jefferson as unconsciously representing legitimate "economic means" in the interest of a society in which most men might apply "labour and capital to natural resources for the production of wealth." Hamilton in this scheme represented the "political means," that is, the interest of the exploiting class who, through adroit use of the machinery of government, appropriated without compensation the labor products of the producer. This artificial and somewhat rigid injection of Beard, Oppenheimer, and Georgite economics comes awkwardly into the narrative. Nor is it quite clear just why Jefferson, head of the Republican party, owner of more than a hundred slaves, and member of the class of large planters, was necessarily more of a producer than a Yankee merchant.[14]

Nock observed that Jefferson was too often concerned with the immediate political bearings of the Hamiltonian system. This unfortunately diverted his attention from the "theoretical economics" involved. Toward the end of Jefferson's life, when he was no longer active in public service and had more time for contemplation, he seemed to recognize that the government had been fashioned to distribute wealth by political rather than economic means—for the "exploitation of one class by another." But even then Jefferson reverted to the old political rhetoric of denouncing monarchist tendencies, apparently without understanding that the absolutism he feared could be effected in a republic quite as easily as in a monarchy.[15]

If Jefferson, as Nock understood him, was relieved to leave public life, so Nock, after his brief lecture on "fundamental economics," was eager to return to his personal Jefferson—the man of philosophical interests and culture, "the radical with Tory manners." Jefferson's educational theories, especially as they undermined his "democratic" reputation, particularly interested Nock. A phrase he never ceased to quote came from Jefferson's plan for selecting students for the state-supported university: "Twenty of the best geniuses," Jefferson advised, should "be raked from the rubbish annually." Here, Nock felt, was a genuine educational theory based on discrimination, on an aristocracy of merit which had nothing in common with the mistaken popular concept of democratic education that was merely indiscriminate. Jefferson's proposals for public schools were intelligently adapted to "the years, capacity and condition of everyone." Nock's only criticism, which he was to develop at some length in a later book, was of Jefferson's naïve notion that literacy was an absolute prerequisite for a free society. Jefferson, Nock charged, never suspected "the ease with which mere literacy is perverted, and that it is therefore quite possible for a literate people to be much more ignorant than an illiterate people—that a people of well-perverted literacy, indeed, is invincibly unintelligent."[16]

Although Jefferson succeeded in founding the University of Virginia, his original plan was compromised. Nock saw Jefferson as representative of the Remnant, compelled to deal with ignorant politicians and Philistine businessmen who had no notion of the value and purpose of education. Nock wondered that the university, given the times and circumstances, fared as well as it did, since it was dedicated to "the satisfaction of non-existent wants and to the promotion of purposes in which no one had any particular interest."[17]

Nock's portrait of a Jefferson profoundly at odds with his society and cherishing values alien to his fellows led logically to a description of Nock's prototype—the superfluous man. Jefferson, for Nock, was an example of what the sovereignty of the individual could mean; Nock never accepted him as a spokesman for the sovereignty of the people. It was not the Jefferson of the Declaration of Independence nor the champion of the equality of men who interested Nock. His Jefferson stood for the freedom of noble men. Very little is said about the nobility of free men. When Nock reviewed Gilbert Chinard's *Thomas Jefferson: The Apostle of Americanism*, he took exception to the description in the subtitle. Jefferson, he wrote, stood for a creed that "should have been Americanism but never was." Contrary to Chinard's view, Jefferson was a *"vox clamantis in deserto*—in the wilderness of revolting greeds and degrading ambitions and flagitious enterprises . . . a voice that will somehow make itself heard by the few who have ears to hear." Nock's understanding of Jefferson seemed to echo Nietzsche's anarchistic sentiment: "Where the State ceaseth there beginneth the man who is not superfluous." Nock's anarchistic tone throughout the review impressed a student of Matthew Arnold, Stuart Sherman, who remarked that Nock's *Jefferson* was written by a man "who was still looking forward to the millennium when we shall all be philosophic anarchists. . . ." It was, however, an anarchist sentiment that was growing increasingly elitist and aloof from the society in which he lived.[18]

"WHY DON'T YOU leave if you dislike it so much in America?" someone once asked Mencken. "Why do people go to zoos?" he retorted. He took pleasure in his disdain and found the tawdry scene "continuously amusing . . . a ribald and endless show." This was not the case with Nock, who had returned from Europe to research *Jefferson* and see it through the press, but could not wait until its publication to return to Brussels. In the summer of 1926 he was scrambling for a steamer, any steamer, "be it a cattle-boat or an oil-tanker, for I am at the limit of endurance." Nock was certain that he could render better service to America abroad than in his own country.[19]

Nock's work on Jefferson illuminated his growing skepticism over the improvement of mankind. He was dismayed that most Americans had no conception of, or even desire for, freedom, but wanted only comfort, profit, and elementary amusement: "Our present population demands but little, and in consideration of that little will cheerfully barter off its major rights." This deplorable acquiescence would "rot down [the] civilization in very short order." Strangely enough, in his view, the contagion had not yet corrupted the Belgians. In Brussels he noted with enthusiasm that politicians justifiably feared the citizens, who loved beauty and held to their traditions with "unbreakable tenacity." Here again is the peculiar logic of elitist anarchism—a love of transcendent traditions but no deference or respect for authority. Nock contended that culture and taste developed organically through freedom. At the same time, in his attempt to explain the absence of any discrimination or appreciation for art and literature in the United States, he pointed, like Henry James, to the absence of institutional apparatus to encourage civilized society and lend prestige to cultural enterprise. Despite his enthusiasm for freedom, Nock lamented the absence of "encysted cultures," institutions, and traditions in America. Europe, he noted, has a church, a state, and a civil service that had encouraged the arts and brought the people to a point at which they could "relish the sublime."[20]

On the surface it seems inconsistent for an anarchist individualist to lament the absence of institutions, usually a restraining influence on the individual. And yet the extreme individualist, to this day, often agrees with the traditional conservative in their longing for community. Nock's utopian dream of a cultured society would not be without order and community standards. But they would develop from within the individual citizen, not be imposed from above by an exploiting and manipulating class. Nor was he alone in his feeling that a European community like Brussels provided an atmosphere of greater freedom and privacy than an American city in the twenties. It is the testimony of countless expatriates of that decade. Nevertheless, Nock's criticism of the state and its restraining institutions seems to have been directed primarily at democratic mass societies where there was great popular influence on community cultural values. Nock's appreciation of Brussels, where class distinctions were more rigid than in America, suggests that he may have longed for an ordered, structured society that gave him security and prestige.

In 1928 Nock published a collection of essays, *On Doing the Right Thing*. Many of them had been written in Europe, but all had appeared in the *American Mercury* and *Harper's Magazine*. The writing lacked the flamboyance of Mencken's swashbuckling, but it is not surprising that many of them found their way into the *Mercury*. Its editors had announced that they were interested in "civilized entertainment" for a specialized audience of "The Forgotten Man: that is, the small group of intelligent citizens who are harassed by cumulative, executive, legislative and judicial follies . . ."—in short, the Remnant.[21]

Nock's association with Mencken developed into a warm friendship. Nock's anarchistic individualism and growing suspicion of majoritarian democracy appealed to Mencken, who called himself a spokesman for "absolute individualism." In addition, his piquant use of English, combining earthy vernacular with eloquent Victorianisms, and his command of the hot flush and hostile snort perfectly suited the *Mercury*. But Nock remained mildly critical of Mencken's occasionally sensational iconoclasm, which failed to expose the fundamental causes of the cultural desert he surveyed. Nock viewed the critical journalism of Mencken and the realism of writers like Sinclair Lewis as often "pseudo-critical," produced by "cheeky reporters with rather nasty minds." Their work seemed to have no purpose beyond its appeal to the smug superiority and complacency "of Little Jack Horner."[22]

Nock designed his cultural criticism as more than an exposé of the Philistine aberrations of American society. He felt that he was genuinely searching for causes and encouraging kindred spirits to seek a more humane life. The aim was noble and intelligent, but the performance was uneven, and the frank elitism of his conclusions was often scarcely different from Mencken's.

In Nock's 1924 references to the Remnant, he was not making a "supercilious discrimination as between, say, the clever and the stupid, or the educated and the uneducated." In these later essays it became increasingly apparent that those who were able "to see things as they are," who had *Intelligenz*, were only those who had received a proper "formative" education similar to Nock's. In contrast to his earlier enthusiasm, he suggested that the "grand average of local taste for the bathos" implanted deep in the soul of the masses made it improbable that many men had either inclination or talent for genuine education. But Nock remained ambivalent over the potential of the average man. On the one hand, he continued to argue that the average taste was educable, but, on the other, that there was no force in society with either the energy or interest to undertake so herculean a task. In the essay "Towards a New Quality-Product" he wistfully entertained the idea that some philanthropist might establish a small college based on Nock's romantic conception of a medieval university. Dedicated to the "grand old fortifying curriculum," it would admit no one who was not prepared to seek genuine formative knowledge instead of vocational training. Its aim would be to produce a quality product. A sympathetic critic suggested that such an institution might "breed a batch of cultivated, sensitive beings who would all die six months after they were exposed to . . . actual civilization." Nock agreed that this was a possibility but, given the alternatives, such an experiment was worth trying. A few years later, in an influential disquisition on education in America, he developed these ideas at much greater length.[23]

Nock's theories concerning the degradation of popular education governed a good deal of his thinking on American civilization in general. The country, he wrote, was methodically turning out a citizenry dedicated to "expansion," by which he meant aggressive commercialism. It produced few men to lead the nation toward other values. As a result the quantity of mass-produced goods in the United States was high, but their quality was low, and the people themselves resembled mass-produced products. This, he felt, could be seen everywhere in

American life. Nock was now more sympathetic to Mumford's argument that the people were victims but did not stress their victimization by an economic system of exploitation as much as he had in the past. What, he wondered, could artists and writers do with the "curiously uniform, undistinguished, characterless quality" of the American population? Dickens, it was true, had dealt with the commonest sort of people in nineteenth-century England, but they, Nock noted, were *"interesting."*[24]

Nock thought it significant that a novelist could find "interesting characters" only among the models furnished by "encysted cultures," which clung with obstinate tenacity to their "traditional bent"—as the Belgians did—and maintained it against the overwhelming "levelling forces" of the democratic society all around them. And yet the fictional characterization of a product of the American melting pot did interest him: for years Nock had nurtured a peculiar enthusiasm for the work of Montague Glass, the author of such Jewish dialect stories as *Potash and Perlmutter*. Brand Whitlock and Nock, who had corresponded since 1912, frequently addressed one another as Abe and Mawruss, the main characters in the stories. Glass's characters were stereotypes of retail salesmen in the needle trade. They were grasping tradesmen who were always on the make; as people, Nock admitted, they were as dreadful as their counterparts in real life—"but what profoundly interesting characters! . . ." In former days he had often used a Dickens character, Murdstone, as a symbol for the materialist culture of nineteenth-century America, but now Murdstone was frequently replaced by Glass's Mr. Finkman. For Nock, Mr. Finkman became the symbol of American cultural life. "This might be thought a delicate matter to press," he wrote, but his sojourns in America had convinced him that Finkman was truly representative. He added that some day a "record-breaking pogrom" would probably take place in New York. Even the most "peace-loving person among us," Nock added, "wishes he could send over for a couple of *sotnias* of Cossacks to floor-manage the subway rush."[25]

Discussing the decline of intelligence and refined conversation, Nock made Mr. Finkman the scapegoat and tastemaker. A supreme occasion, to Finkman, is dinner at his partner's home, where after dinner "all the evening until midnight we sit and talk it business."

The moment one charts the civilization, Nock wrote, one sees the line set by Mr. Finkman. His "tastes and distastes" have great influence on America and are the "principal lead" for any scholar interested in fathoming the depths of the Philistine wastelands. Under Nock's sarcasm, Mr. Finkman bore the burden of all that was crass and acquisitive in American life. When Finkman talked business, which, according to Nock, was all that he was capable of, "the value of ideas, ideals, opinions, sentiments, [was] purely quantitative." Finkman knew and appreciated "instrumental knowledge" because he had "established the American formula of success." To Nock, Mr. Finkman had become a twentieth-century Horatio Alger in a more insidious guise. Nock said that he was not complaining or carping; the Finkmans should have their day. They might prove that men can live full lives "without intellect, without beauty, without religion and morals, and with but the most rudimentary social life," provided they were free to pursue their instinct for expansion. If so, Nock remarked, Finkman would have the laugh on men who still held the quaint notion that "the whole course of human history" denied such a possibility. Finkman's experiment is "the great American experiment" and from a purely detached, disinterested point of view, Nock observed, was well worth watching.[26]

Given the climate of the twenties, when racist ideology was spreading, when a new edition of Madison Grant's *The Passing of the Great Race* sold extremely well, and when the growing power and influence of the Ku Klux Klan could be seen, from rural hamlets to national party-convention halls, Nock's exploitation of Glass's rather harmless stories cannot be dismissed lightly. It is ironic that Nock, critic of a civilization marked by "an extraordinary and inquisitional intolerance of the individual and a corresponding insistence upon conformity to pattern," should resort to stereotyped ethnic imagery to advance the cause of culture and right thinking. The sometimes subdued and sometimes blatant anti-Semitism of the literary intelligentsia of the twenties has been carefully documented. It is not easy to see how Nock differed substantially from the writers he charged with pandering to "vague malevolences, suspicions, repugnances." His ethnic slurs were perhaps not as overt as Mencken's anti-Semitic outbursts. Nevertheless it is difficult to see how Nock's use of such methods discouraged the forces of ignorance and provincialism to which he was presumably opposed.[27]

It would be unfair to suggest that Nock's criticism of mass democracy and its Philistine culture rested solely on such disaffections. The Finkmans were for Nock what the Snopeses were for Faulkner, and despite the unfortunate implications of the choice, his criticism was directed at an entire society given over to the acquisitive instinct for expansion. In such an aggressive, anxious society the only relief lay in childish amusements and counterfeit culture. There was an "enormous army of commercial enterprisers engaged in pandering" to the lowest common denominator and employing every "conceivable device of ingenuity to confirm and flatter and reassure it. Publishers, newspaper-proprietors, editors, preachers, purveyors of commercial amusement, college presidents—the list [was] endless."[28]

There was in Nock, as there is today among critics of mass culture, an ambivalence; he wavered between the view that there is a deliberate manipulative conspiracy to degrade public taste and the view that the masses are innately incapable of appreciating anything but vulgar, shoddy goods. The former is the position of a radical who insists that privileged power, fearing imagination and creative thought, deliberately desires to keep the quality of education, and thus of taste, at a low level in order to insure a docile, gullible citizenship. The latter view is that of an aristocrat who sees taste, culture, and refinement as the private property of an elite threatened by barbarian, democratic hordes who demand only pseudo culture—bread and circuses. The radical and the elitist meet in their common denunciation of popular culture, but they are diametrically opposed when they point to its source. Mencken for example, was firmly convinced that a boob was indeed a boob; it was an absurd and dangerous illusion even to think that one could raise the level of his cultural standards. A radical, on the other hand, like the earlier Nock, was certain that by overthrowing the entire economic and political system a new life would be achieved in which everyone would have time to develop his instinctive taste for excellence.

By the late twenties Nock's position was ambiguous. In the *Freeman* he had repeatedly reminded critics of American culture that the

"politicians, war makers, journalists and the like" corrupted the wholesome and instinctively good sense of the average taste. Carping
critics, he had written, should abandon their superficial descriptions
of mass culture's absurdities and "help liberate average reason and
average taste so that they may function freely and naturally." Apparently he now found such a view hopelessly utopian: the educational
system was not deliberately degraded but designed to meet the demands of an aggressively ignorant populace. Success, or recognition
by the mob, had become the governing obsession and even imaginative, talented writers, if they wished to belong to the society, had to
cater to the oppressive popular taste.[29]

During Nock's tenure as literary critic for the *Freeman*, his dispar-
agement of younger writers and his censure of critics for their destructive irresponsibility often sounded like the strictures of the Humanist scholars, led by two survivors of the "genteel tradition," Irving
Babbitt and Paul Elmer More. Burton Rascoe, a persistent scoffer at
the Humanists, wrote caustically that "the Babbitts and the Paul Elmer
Mores, the Brownells all had the hall marks of that culture on which
Mr. Nock prides himself and his generation; but it was to the younger
generation ashes in the mouth." Nock agreed but insisted that it was
not his generation's cultural training that was at fault but the failure
of such beneficiaries of that training as Babbitt and More to realize
that "it was not enough to have culture, but that one must have the
passion to make it prevail."[30]

During his time on the *Freeman* Nock had seldom mentioned either
Babbitt or More, and it is unlikely that an infusion of radical economics and social science into his literary judgments would have been
acceptable to those conservatives. The common ground between Nock
and the Humanists was their insistence on the efficaciousness of a
classical literary training and their contempt for nearly all modern
literature. But Nock's humanitarianism was abhorrent to them. His
missionary zeal to bring culture to the populace at large must have
appeared as absurd to the elitist Humanists as it did to one of their
most vitriolic critics, H. L. Mencken. Nock saw himself as a bearer of
culture to the masses; the Humanists saw themselves as guardians of
culture against the masses. Nevertheless, with Nock's retreat from

weekly journalism into the world of biography and reflective cultural analysis, his views of modern culture increasingly seemed to be in the Humanist vein.

What was often called the New Humanism was hardly new. Its chief spokesmen, Babbitt and More, had since the first years of the century been applying their profound knowledge of the literature of antiquity to literary and cultural criticism. Custodians of classical culture against the menacing inroads of modernist thought, they had written a score of scholarly books that had great influence within the academy.[31] But New Humanism did not coalesce into a movement until the late twenties. In 1930 Professor Norman Foerster published an anthology of essays called *Humanism and America*. It was soon given a vigorous rebuttal by *The Critique of Humanism*, an essay collection edited by a liberal biographer and political historian, C. Hartley Grattan. The battle involved writers from diverse groups and from two or three literary generations. Malcolm Cowley, an acerbic critic of the Humanists, has pointed out that while the issues were often confused, they clearly involved not only artistic and aesthetic but also moral and political questions, primarily concerning the role of the artist and his moral obligation to society.[32]

In the world of art and culture, as in life itself, the Humanists stood for tradition much in the manner of Edmund Burke opposing Jean Jacques Rousseau and Thomas Paine. They spoke for the "wisdom of the ages" rather than for the "wisdom of the age." They sought stability, continuity, and order as a contrast to the prevailing romanticism and standardless humanitarianism of those whom they scornfully described as the "philosophers of the flux, or, in the phrase of Aristophanes, votaries of the God Whirl." For More the real question was "not whether there are standards but whether they shall be based on tradition or shall be struck out brand new by each successive generation or by each individual critic."[33]

Modernism, however, strained against classical tradition and authoritarian controls, challenged established forms and decorum, and accepted new ideas. It saw the low, mean, distasteful, and grotesque as fit subject matter for the artist. To the Humanists the chief modernist heresies were naturalism and romanticism. The chief heretics were Francis Bacon for his naturalistic, scientific positivism and Rousseau for his sentimental yet dangerous romanticism. Their crime and that of their deluded followers was that through naturalism they had equated man with nature and looked on him as a creature governed solely by nature's laws, which were expansive, materialistic, and apart from human values. Through romanticism, they had encouraged the free play of natural instincts, encouraged man's bestial impulses, and turned his animality into high virtue. For the Humanist a fundamental duality existed. There was a "law for man" and a "law for thing." Man's lower instincts often succumbed to the law of nature, but through cultivation of his higher self he could curb them. More believed that the artist "is aware indeed of the bestial in man, but sees also something else, and in that something else looks for the meaning of life." Central to Humanist critical perspective was the conviction that the artist's moral and critical faculties must be in harmony.[34]

"The proper study of mankind is man," Foerster maintained, and by studying the Great Tradition men would be able to perceive and realize their humanity. There they would discover the basic human law—identified by the Humanists as the "Law of Measure," "Golden Mean," "Inner Check," "Vital Control," renunciation, "Veto Power," restraint, discipline, and decorum. By the practice of these virtues— inspired by and in imitation of the great models of antiquity—man could ultimately attain poise, a sense of proportion, and what Babbitt described as "the end of ends," sublime individual happiness.[35]

Humanist philosophy called for an interior spiritual regeneration with which Nock could sympathize. Humanists were interested in "a *kind* of culture, a kind of literature, a kind of psychological and moral effect," a "Christian kind of conduct" that always appealed to Nock despite his abandonment of the church and orthodoxy. Babbitt, like Nock, claimed that he detested organized religion, but he was a profoundly religious man. More, who retained his scholarly skepticism, became an eminent Anglican thinker. It is doubtful that Humanism would have been so vital if it had not had an otherworldly religious perspective. T. S. Eliot, who walked a tightrope between Humanism and modernism, was inclined to think that Humanism without religion would be a frail reed. In any event, the religious overtones of Humanism did not clash with Nock's clerical background and private sense of religiosity.[36]

Nock and the Humanists were dismayed by contemporary society's lowly acquisitive aspirations and by an educational system bent on training at the expense of knowledge. He also mused, like some of the Humanists, on the possibility of establishing a separate university for those interested in the "grand old fortifying curriculum." He abandoned the idea on the ground that there were not enough scholars of the great tradition to staff such an institution—which might indicate that he was not entirely captivated by Humanist promises.[37]

Nock could appreciate the antidemocratic exasperation of the Humanists who saw democracy as dedicated only to the elevation of mediocrity. With his own reliance on the Saving Remnant, a term Babbitt also took from Arnold, Nock could look with approval on More's demand for a natural aristocracy not based on inherited wealth and "the crude dominion of money." Nor was the Humanist criticism of humanitarianism as sentimental sympathy for "mankind in the lump" at the expense of individuality and self-reform antithetical to Nock's gradual disillusionment with all forms of collective social reform and his belief that the best one could do was tend one's own garden. Finally, Nock's warm appreciation for what he described as the encysted culture and traditions of Belgium suggests that he, like so many of the Humanists, was in search of a society whose institutions deferred to men of refinement and taste. With the Humanist critique of contemporary society Nock was in general agreement.[38]

There was, however, a profound, decisive difference in temperament between the Humanist doctrine of restraint and Nock's anarchical individualism. The philosophy of Humanist morality was profoundly negative. The Humanists agreed with Joseph Joubert that morality was "formed only to repress and constrain; . . . morality is a bridle and not a spur." This concept prompted them to see the Puritans as examples of inner discipline and moral restraint. Nock, however, who believed that the Puritans had persistently violated natural instinct to the detriment of human potential, indicted Puritanism as a "cancerous interest in the personal conduct of others." Nock believed with the Humanists that there were two sides to man, "one divine and the other bestial." But even after he had come to see the bestial as prevailing, he asserted, along with his friend Edward Epstean, that "an energetic strengthening" of the divine was far more worthwhile than efforts to "repress and weaken" the bestial: "Repression is negative, enervating. Put all your work on the positive job."[39]

Such a staunch defender of personal privacy as Nock would not discuss, and certainly would not censure, Goethe, as Babbitt did, for engaging in love affairs when well into his seventies. To Babbitt this suggested that Goethe was deficient in austerity. If Nock had an opinion, he probably would have found Goethe's behavior inspiring. There is nothing in Nock remotely similar to More's lament over the decadence of the "New Morality" with its sensual music and "exaggeration of sex in the clothing." In 1915 Nock, who ridiculed prudish ministers for always wanting to close something down while it was his idea "always to open something," wrote: "I saw [a pretty Frenchwoman] at Porquerolles, a copper blonde about twenty-five years old. Her copper tint was authentic, for when she raised her arms she showed great tufts of hair of the same shade. I have often wondered why a depilated armpit is repulsive to me." So much for the Victorian fastidiousness that separated the Humanists from Nock and prompted his boisterous friend Mencken to brand them "intolerant crepe-clad pundits."[40]

Temperamentally alien to Nock was Humanism's preoccupation with morality, its interest in repressing spontaneity, and its aversion to joy, "especially the joys of other people." Even during his most despairing last years, he remained a sophisticated cosmopolitan. It is not surprising that the humanism of the "New Humanists" never embraced Rabelais, in whom Nock found his highest inspiration.[41]

This temperamental distinction carried over into their critical judgment of men and events. The Humanist "inner check" was easier to name than define. More candidly admitted the difficulty when he wrote: "What, if anything, lies behind the inner check, what it is, why and how it acts or neglects to act, we cannot express in rational terms." Such vagueness meant that when the Humanists got down to specific issues, they invariably discovered that what lay behind the inner check were the traditional institutions of authority and social control. More's search for a way to insure the selection of a natural aristocratic leadership is a case in point. He hoped that it might come from "social consciousness," but he was willing to settle for "some form of machinery" that would provide for the selection of "the best" and the "bestowal on them of 'power'; it is the true consummation of democracy." The phrase "some form of machinery" would surely have aroused Nock's anarchical suspicion. Nock could never have found More's assertion, "to the civilized man *the rights of property are more important than the right to life*," acceptable to his Georgite notions that "man is a land animal" (a statement repugnant to any Humanist) and that the essence of democracy is public ownership.[42] In discussing aristocracy and justice, More invariably defends privileged property, while Nock even in his last years argued that genuine democracy depended on the diffusion of property. Nock was far too skeptical to accept the utopianism of Babbitt, who complacently announced that "the remedy for the evils of competition" was to be found "in the magnanimity of the strong and successful, and not in any sickly sentimentalizing over the lot of the underdog." Although Nock was soon to denounce his own former sympathy for the "prolotoorios," he never adopted Babbitt's faith in the potential virtues of the rich and powerful. Alfred Kazin's statement—that More was "always more worshipful of Oxford than any Oxonian, and a gratuitous defender of aristocracy"— would apply as well to Babbitt and most of the Humanists.[43]

In America, lacking royalty and established traditions, the Humanists looked on the Puritans and their government as the nation's best example of moral, aristocratic leadership—an example from which the country had unfortunately descended. Nock, coming to his interpretation through the influence of such progressive historians as Beard, Turner, and Becker, argued that Puritan political organization had been little more than a merchant-state designed to allow one class to exploit another. As for their religious motives and established church, these had proved to be the effective tools of a confiscatory state. Nock approved of the fragmented and decentralized power of the states under the Articles of Confederation and saw the Constitution as a coup d'état of scheming manipulators, but Babbitt valued the Constitution as a properly Burkian document establishing unity, authority, and control. Nock would have looked with contempt on Babbitt's defense of the Supreme Court as the "ethical basis" of American government and "more than any other institution the higher or permanent self of the State." The court, in Nock's view, was the bulwark of a corrupt state, and the "nine old crates" who staffed it served its insidious, exploitive designs. Babbitt's insistence that in order to save society from barbarism and anarchy it was necessary to "substitute the doctrine of the right man for the doctrine of the rights of man" smacked of an aristocratic authoritarianism that was hardly congenial to Nock.[44]

At the core of the difference between Nock and the Humanists was the anarchical antiauthoritarianism of his growing elitism. Babbitt's attack on Jeffersonianism for its faith in "the goodness of natural man" would not have bothered Nock, who had grown increasingly skeptical of that optimistic notion. But Babbitt's easy acceptance of external authority, a "veto power either in the individual" or, if necessary, "in the State," was repugnant to Nock. There was in Humanism what Allen Tate described as "a kind of moral Fascism." Alfred Kazin has noted how easily Humanists like Seward Collins could move from the Humanist camp to a belief in "Fascism run by gentlemen." It is to the point that Collins and Stuart Sherman, at one time a leading Humanist critic, recognized a fundamental anarchistic impulse in Nock, which placed him outside Humanist conservatism. It is interesting that Babbitt's words for the potential horror of modernist trends were "anarchy," "anarchical individualism," and "anarchical impressionism."[45]

Nock, like the Humanists, was in search of an internal moral and even spiritual regeneration, but the quality of his search was individualistic. It had an existential quality, for it was seen as a tremendous burden to be undertaken alone. Such personal integrity, such authenticity, was possible, he felt at that point of his life, only by escaping into the company of kindred spirits, far from the influence of deadening institutions. The Humanists, far more political, distrusted such isolated passivity. More upbraided Thoreau for cutting "himself off from the Church and the State" and failing to remain in "the greater currents of tradition." Babbitt's warning might have been addressed to Nock; he wrote that anyone "who puts his faith in the divinity of the average is destined . . . to pass through disillusion to final despair."[46]

There was, Nock felt, very little that one could do: "I was never much for evangelization," he claimed. Even if an opportunity arose to bring about change, he would not take it. He thought that spiritual regeneration was never achieved through revolutions but only through individual regeneration. At any rate, Nock no longer seemed to believe that a sincere critic had to be constructive or that he could transform character. The minds of the mass of Americans, he observed, were obviously not fitted to the kind of changes he might advocate. His message was one of passive resignation and watchful waiting. To expect to work from within society was as futile as expecting a YMCA director to run a brothel: "He might trim off some of the coarser fringes . . . and put things in . . . a state of 'outward order and decency,' but he *must* run an assignation-house, or he would promptly hear from the owners."[47]

Despite his gloomy view, Nock still anticipated relief in some distant future. Finkman's experiment was ultimately doomed. Members of the Remnant were presently superfluous, but they still had an "invincible ally on their side—the self-preserving instinct in humanity." In "A Cultural Forecast" Nock refused to predict just when this instinct might reassert itself, but he was confident that it would, for "it always does. Ignorance, vulgarity, a barbaric and superficial spirit may, and from all appearances will, predominate unquestioned for years in America [and] no one can set a term on it. But a term there is, nevertheless." Men would return to the humane life because they could not do without it. In the meantime Nock advised those of the surviving Remnant to emulate Pascal and stay quietly in their chambers.[48]

It may seem paradoxical that an advocate of passive resignation, the spokesman for an increasingly elitist view of society, should continue stoutly to maintain his anarchism. But this is not without precedent in American intellectual history. His position was like that of Emerson and Thoreau, apostles of anarchical perfectionism in the 1830s and 1840s. The anarchist individualism of those earlier rebels became the anarchist elitism of men like Albert Jay Nock. Emerson's "American Scholar" can be read as the statement of a radical philosophic anarchism that demands withdrawal, detachment, and freedom for the disinterested man—Man Thinking. Much like Thoreau, who had preached and practiced a self-contained existence in order to show the world the fatuousness of collective enterprise, Nock insisted on complete autonomy for the individual isolated from society; only with such autonomy could corruption be avoided.[49]

The clearest, most articulate statement of Nock's anarchist faith may be found in two essays, "Anarchist's Progress" and the title essay of *On Doing the Right Thing*. The first was a nostalgic account of his early life and education combined with an attack on politics, politicians, and the state. He returned to Oppenheimer's arguments, supported by quotations from Jefferson, the physiocrats, and other classic exponents of laissez faire. "On Doing the Right Thing" was an eloquent defense of philosophical anarchism. Nock saw both essays as presenting "something . . . in the way of a personal story of [his] anarchist philosophy and its development." In both he struggled to reconcile his growing elitism with the humanitarian perfectionism that lay at the bottom of the anarchist vision.[50]

The deeply moralistic element in anarchism has always made it more than a political doctrine. "On Doing the Right Thing" presents the anarchist ethical and moral code. Essentially this involves acknowledging that men only do the right thing when they are free to make choices. Every enlargement of government activity limits the areas of individual choice, and as they become limited so do human dignity, conscience, and individual responsibility. "Want of liberty, by strengthening law and decorum, stupefies conscience," declared Emerson, in a defense of anarchic individualism. Thoreau found that men dictated to by external coercion exhibited "no free exercise whatever of the judgment of the moral sense." Nock continued in this tradition, holding that the state inevitably encouraged the destruction of moral fiber by usurping the role of a man's conscience. It gradually brought him in peril of not recognizing in his conscience what was required of him. Ultimately the distinction between right and wrong action would be obliterated.[51]

Emerson lamented that "individualism has never been tried." Nock echoed the sentiment when he defended the anarchist's moral vision: "In suggesting that we try freedom . . . the anarchist and individualist has a strictly practical aim. He aims at the production of a race of responsible beings." Nock contended that a man has an absolute right to conduct his personal life in a manner judged disreputable by prevailing standards. Endorsing Benjamin Tucker's insistence on "the right of the drunkard, the gambler, the rake, and the harlot to live their lives until they shall freely choose to abandon them," Nock felt that genuine freedom meant the right "to go on without any code of morals at all." It also meant the freedom to "rationalise, construct and adhere to a code of one's own." Where there was no free choice there was no freedom. The constant invasion of legalism and authoritarianism into matters of personal conduct and conscience undermined even the possibility of moral education.[52]

In the twenties prohibition and legal restrictions on sexual relations seemed the most obvious invasions of privacy. To Nock, both areas were outside the realm of law. But he was not interested in merely attacking the hypocrisy of the blue laws or the absurdities of Comstockery. He did not see himself as a defender of avant-garde, Bohemian libertarianism. On the contrary, he was distressed by the exploitation of raw sensation and the example of lives lived "from one squalid little *Schweinerei* to another." But he still thought that absolute freedom to pursue such degradation allowed also for the freedom to pursue higher, more decent lives and thereby develop, through self-discipline, human dignity and integrity. "The anarchist," he wrote, keeps before him the "practical object, *i.e.,* that men may become as good and decent, as elevated and noble, as they might be and really wish to be." Nock still claimed that reason and experience convinced him that men could and would "educate themselves to this desirable end." As long as their lives were shaped and dominated by legalism and authoritarianism, they never could.[53]

Nock's "moral anarchism" was at one with his attack on the state. He viewed the Philistine conformity and vulgarization of values in a mass society and culture as permanent features of the state apparatus. He was extremely sensitive to what has come to be seen by many as the essence of the twentieth-century revolution—the development of a planned economy, the centralization of power, and the managerial revolution. Nock warned against the leveling effect of industrial technocracy, sophisticated mass communications, and organizational technique. He predicted mass uniformity as one of the most menacing developments in Western society. An individual in a great, transcendent society would become little more than an interchangeable part; even leaders would become victims, shaped, molded, and directed by the leviathan state, which seemed to have a life of its own. Nock's revolt against such standardization and dehumanization was solidly in the mainstream of traditional anarchist individualist dissent. It has been and remains the noblest part of the anarchist creed.[54]

George Woodcock, in his admirable study of anarchism, observed that anarchists' "ruthless criticism of the present was always [their] great strength." Albert Jay Nock's work is no exception. In the essays written in the twenties Nock perceived the potentially destructive course of progress, in its development of a mass-citizenry, whose life would be subject to ever greater scrutiny and control. The uninteresting faces that Nock observed all about him in the twenties were to become David Riesman's "lonely crowd" and C. Wright Mills's passive hordes of the fifties and sixties—never questioning, never looking back, registering their feelings over the counter, counted, computed, graphed, and indexed. Nock saw Whitman's "Democratic Vistas" realized, "man viewed in the lump." "Shall a man," asked Whitman, "lose himself in countless masses of adjustments, and be so shaped with reference to this, that, and the other, that the simply good and healthy and brave parts of him are reduced and clipped away, like the bordering of a box in a garden?" Nock's essays reflect Whitman's fears and at the same time anticipate the despair of anarchistic critic Dwight Macdonald, who writes of the twentieth-century mass-man as nonman, "man forced into a relationship with other men that makes it impossible for him to function as a man." Nock's foreboding suggests the inevitable development of a race with no private life, no personal desires, and no hobbies, aspirations, or aversions that are not shared by everyone else.[55]

These Orwellian views cannot be dismissed as the inevitable disillusionment of a naïve anarchist whose faith in human perfectibility has been shattered. Nock raised the fundamental question: How can men remain men in a mass society? Neither his protest nor any before or since has offered much in the way of a tangible program of escape. The anarchist distrusts programs, systems, organization, and compulsion. The politics of the antipolitical cuts the anarchist off from a society where power means manipulation. Nock spoke for the individual who refused to be manipulated. In the midst of his century the preservation of personal identity seems even more crucial than it was in Whitman's time. To enlarge the area in which personal, individual, human values can operate remains the task of thinking man.

Nock saw this as the fundamental obligation of a critic. However, he spoke more and more to and for the Remnant, believing that in an increasingly small minority lay the only hope of the future. His revolt against the wave of the future was, like that of many "conscience stricken gentlemen" drawn to anarchist movements, both millennial and nostalgic. He spoke of a future when men would return to the humane life; and he looked to an ideal past for examples. The natural, spontaneous, individual spirit has in all times been a rarity, but Nock felt that it was becoming an impossibility. The anarchist rebellion was not necessarily in favor of the past, as George Woodcock has observed, but it was for an ideal that belonged outside the present in which the anarchists found themselves. Nock believed in the idea of progress, but not in progress as it was conceived by modern industrial society; moral progress was only possible through individual self-realization and regeneration.[56]

Nock rarely had a good word for organized religion. It was no more than another of society's external institutions that restrained and distorted individuality. He did, however, credit it with making the best use of the rejuvenating power of pilgrimages. During the years of his essays on American culture and the articles recording his "anarchist's progress," he had also taken an intellectual pilgrimage to the life, work, and civilization of "one of the world's great libertarians," the Pantagruelist, François Rabelais.[57]

In 1929 Nock published, in collaboration with Catherine Rose Wilson, a book-length essay, *Francis Rabelais: The Man and His Work*. It later served as the introduction to a two-volume annotated edition of the eighteenth-century English translation of Rabelais by Sir Thomas Urquhart and Peter Motteux that Nock brought out in 1931. With his close friend Ruth Robinson, Nock also made several extended journeys to the provinces of France where Rabelais had lived and worked. The trips resulted in a charming travel book, *Journey into Rabelais's France*, illustrated by Miss Robinson with pen and ink drawings perfectly attuned to the gaiety and rollicking humor of the text.[58]

Van Wyck Brooks called *Francis Rabelais* Nock's own *Mont-Saint-Michel and Chartres*, his homage to his "best-beloved human type and the epoch in which he would have felt at home." It was indeed a pilgrimage and a profound experience that brought him a joy that endured throughout his life. But Nock's intellectual return to sixteenth-century France was not very much like Henry Adams's retreat into the Middle Ages. Adams was drawn to that past because he believed it so irrevocably distinct from his own time. Nock, on the contrary, turned to a study of Rabelais and his times because he found them so relevant to the modern world.[59]

In an address to the medical faculty of Johns Hopkins University Nock extolled the great achievements of Rabelais the physician. Then, speaking of Rabelais's time, Nock developed a series of remarkable comparisons: "It was a period more nearly like ours than any other in history. The difficulties and temptations that the human spirit faced" were the same. There was a revolution in industry, and commerce had inflated avarice into a mania. Despite misconceptions, religious conviction played as little part in the conduct of public life as it does now. Then, as now, a ruinous centralization had encouraged the rise of a bureaucratic "bourgeois of bankers, speculators, shavers, lawyers, jobholders," and men of the robe intent on exploitation and appropriation. For these reasons, said Nock, Rabelais "was particularly a man of our own time." His wonderful quality of spirit developed in spite of circumstances as unfavorable as those confronting a sensitive person today. Nock hoped that renewed contact with Rabelais might offer inspiration to the beleaguered twentieth-century men of spirit.[60]

Although Nock returned to the example of Rabelais for comfort and inspiration, he did not look with longing on the sixteenth century as Henry Adams had on the twelfth. Rabelais, to Nock, was not like the Virgin to Henry Adams. Rabelais was the Nockian hero par excellence—an alienated spokesman for the Remnant. His writings were directed at a special order of imaginative and kindred spirits. All of Rabelais's work displayed "his enduring affinity with the alien spirits, of whom there are always some in every society, who at any sacrifice resist, or rather, quietly elude, all pressure towards conformity, towards standardization and mechanization of thought, sentiment or belief." Nock's appreciation of Rabelais was remarkably like that of Anatole France, who wrote that despite what had been said of it, "*Pantagruel* is a work written solely for the lettered; Pantagruelism is a philosophy accessible only to the elite of rare minds; it is almost an esoteric doctrine, hidden and secret." This was exactly how Nock understood the work of his hero.[61]

It was not necessary for Nock to remake Rabelais into his own image as he had done with Jefferson. He reveled in the writing of Rabelais, a genuine kindred spirit. His work lost much of its previous petulance and took on a gay and joyous cynicism or, as Rabelais put it, "a certain jollity of mind, pickled in the scorn of fortune." Nock particularly admired Rabelais's equanimity, which he believed was born of a sense of superiority: "That is the right word," he wrote, "a gay, joyous, wise, imaginative, tolerant superiority." Rabelais's character, the hermit of St. Radegonde, had been instilled with his creator's spirit. "One perceives," Nock wrote, "that he knew human nature rather well and did not expect too much of it, so doubtless he lived in the equanimity that is born of that wisdom and one has a comfortable feeling about him. Peace and repose be his."[62]

Nock's admiration for Rabelais involves an almost revelatory experience. Nock was certain that Rabelais had learned from "the blessed apostle" that "one must suffer fools gladly." He wondered at "how easily the great Pantagruelists seem to do that, but it only seems easy, it really is very hard to do. How easily, how exquisitely, Rabelais did it." For Nock, Pantagruelism was like Christianity. Indeed, Rabelais's writings seem to have served Nock as the Scriptures have served others. Reading Rabelais, he recalled, had sustained and supported his spirit for years: "I could not possibly have got through without him."[63]

It is not surprising that Nock should vigorously reject the interpretation of scholars who saw in Rabelais a brilliant polemicist. Nock was sure that Rabelais's work was never meant as political allegory or satire. A satirist was indignant, involved, a partisan. The Pantagruelist, on the contrary, never became preoccupied with the success of a cause or deluded himself by anticipating anything worthwhile from its triumph. Zealousness and commitment to an immediate program led not only to disappointment but usually to a new form of tyranny. The Pantagruelist, to be sure, was a critic of his times and institutions, but he never stooped to rail at the triviality of human pretensions, nor did he recommend the humane life: he merely lived it. Through his actions the good and worthwhile life "shows itself as something lovely and infinitely desirable, by the side of which all other attainments fall automatically into their proper place as cheap, poor, and trivial."[64]

Nock found in Rabelais's *Lives, Heroick Deeds, and Sayings of Gargantua and His Sonne Pantagruel* the essence of the humanism that was the core of his own philosophical anarchism. After his victory in the Picrocholean War, the good king Grangousier, father of Gargantua, offered to build a monastery for his faithful warrior, Friar John of the Funnels, "a right monk, if ever there were any, since the monking world monked a monkery." Friar John was to be in charge, but he declined all authority. However, he accepted the Abbey of Thélème, which was to be designed and run after his own fancy. Only one rule was to be observed there: "Do what thou wilt." The abbey was to be dedicated not to ascetic discipline but to absolute individual freedom. There were to be no walls. The inmates might leave at will. Neither bells nor clocks would routinize and deny the spontaneity of life. Members of the abbey might arise, study, and play when they wished. Women were to be enthusiastically admitted, but only in the company of men. Men and women might live together, but marriage was neither demanded nor prohibited. If a man left the abbey he was expected to take his mistress with him. Economic freedom was guaranteed by an ample endowment from the good king Grangousier.[65]

While Nock took great delight in Rabelais's fantasy, he stressed the seriousness of the utopia. One doesn't live in a monastery as Rabelais did for many years, Nock wrote, without learning something "of the ennobling power of freedom." Here was a vision that deserved serious reflection: "The lover of freedom, the disbeliever in a dull and vicious mechanization and standardization of society, with its consequent deformation of the human spirit, its debasement and vulgarization of life's abiding values, will nowhere find a more abundant consolation and encouragement" than in the Pantagruelist vision of the Abbey of Thélème.[66]

The exclusiveness of the abbey should not be neglected. It admitted only a select inner circle of spirits noble in mind as well as body.

The women must be fair, well featured, and of sweet disposition—no "crooked, ill favored, misshapen fools, senseless, spoiled or corrupt." There were to be "no sickly men . . . ill bred louts, simple sots or peevish trouble-houses." All candidates were to be well prepared; there were to be none among them who could not "read, write, sing, play upon several musical instruments, speak five or six several languages, and compose in them all very quaintly, both in verse and prose." The abbey appealed to Nock as an exquisite sanctuary for the noble order of the Remnant. Composed of free men and women, wellborn and well-bred, it was for Nock an elitist-anarchist dream of what absolute freedom could mean, "a portrayal of all that human society might be if only human beings were free to become as good, kind, enlightened, gentle, generous, as they know they can be, and really wish to be."[67]

But it was for Nock more than an eloquent affirmation of the potential of human achievement; it was also a sanctuary for noble spirits from "vile bigots, hypocrites, externally devoted apes," and all the undesirable refuse of humanity who were shut out of an earthly paradise in which "Grace, honour, praise, delight / Here sojourn day and night." The abbey might be a fantasy, but to Nock its spirit rang true. It was a sanctuary for the elevated mind. He might never find an Abbey of Thélème, but he was sure that a man could find within himself the nobility and equanimity he needed. Pantagruelism was more than being able to see the world for what it really was; it was a prescription against infection by the world. In that noble minority endowed with wisdom and grace, aliens in the modern world or any world, Pantagruelism would inspire the will and resolution to maintain the integrity of their individuality "free, superior to chance and circumstance, immune to every debilitating contagion of the mass-mind."[68]

"I have often thought that I might have made a pretty consistent Christian," Nock once wrote, "if it had not been for just that one thing that the blessed Apostle said about suffering fools gladly." Pantagruelism presented a challenging discipline, Nock felt, and offered the only escape from bitterness and rancorous misanthropy. He believed that it alone could point the way to maintaining a vision tempered by shrewdness but unscarred by cynicism. It demanded a religious faith, not in practice or creed but in man's inner resources, to withstand the oppression of ignoble circumstance. For Nock, Pantagruelism embraced the humanistic perfectionism of the anarchist dream while recognizing the elitist necessities demanded by the world.[69]

6. The Revelation
of Cram

Nock's mood of gentlemanly resignation was not a unique response to a society that William C. Bullitt described as totally without "gaiety and without earnestness, mechanical, content, indifferent." Nock was part of a widespread revolt that involved New Humanists from the right and romantic radicals from the left, who found common cause in repudiating the Philistinism of America's commercial society. The degradation of civilization that was epitomized by the Rotarian buffoonery of Harding and Coolidge and climaxed by the platitudes of Hoover provoked the intellectual community, which had never felt so impotent, into some form of defiance. But for many writers and journalists, and Nock was no exception, the defiance was antipolitical, individual, and, more often than not, negative and passive. They seemed to hope that barbarism would run its course.[1]

Escape from the world may have been behind Nock's determination to stand above and apart from the debilitating contagions of the mass mind. Nock seemed to be drawn toward the position that Walter Lippmann took in *A Preface to Morals* (1929), in which Lippmann abandoned his former enthusiastic support of modernism to move away from political conviction. Whereas he had once welcomed the breakdown of conservative orthodoxy and tradition, he now lamented the destruction of "ancient habits" and charged the earlier emancipators with failing to see beyond the evils against which they had rebelled. Lippmann supported the position that Nock had come to accept, that the intellectual should totally withdraw from contemporary affairs, that the mature man should give up his illusions and become "free of that tension which vain expectations beget." By renouncing foolish hopes one could also avoid despair and achieve the superiority of perception that Nock described in his study of Rabelais. The "detached intellectual," unplagued by doubt, ambition, frustration, and fear, could move easily through life, Lippmann wrote. And so, whether he saw it as comedy, tragedy, or farce, he would affirm that the wise man can enjoy it: "Here was true equanimity pickled in the scorn of fortune."[2]

On the other hand, Nock was not unreceptive to Mencken's raucous polemics. It was not merely that Nock appreciated the marvelous ridicule; Mencken's rhetorical barrage contributed greatly to undermining faith in the democratic system, particularly when faith rested on belief in the possibility of informed public opinion. To many, democracy as practiced in America seemed ineffective, incompatible with high standards, to which it was unalterably opposed. The assumption of the three preceding decades that "culture could be democratized without being vulgarized" had proved false. Mencken scorned the very idea of self-government, for popular government had produced prohibition, the Ku Klux Klan, and censorship. To him, the boorishness of the mass mind was as apparent in the swinish rich as in the anthropoid rabble.[3]

Disillusionment with democracy had been encouraged by the development of popular education under the professional educators. By the 1930s they had gained great power and influence not only in elementary and secondary schools but in colleges and universities as well. Their exploitation of the child-centered philosophy of the progressives, it was charged, had turned institutions of higher learning into training schools for adolescents. In 1930 Abraham Flexner launched a devastating assault in his comparative study *Universities: American, English, and German.* Marshaling absurdities, he pictured fatuous pedagogy, insidious commercialism, and inane public service advanced by educational administrators who were proof against Mencken's mordant wit. Universities, in their insane desire to cater to the mob, did nearly everything but educate. They trained expectant housewives to wash dishes more efficiently, offered courses in advertising layout to hopeful Horatio Algers, organized such fields of research as "methods of experimental and comparative cookery," and encouraged such contributions to knowledge as "An Analysis of Janitor Service in Elementary Schools." In this mad attempt to serve ever greater numbers, Flexner charged, the educational bureaucracy had lost sight of the purpose of a university: culture could not flourish in the "feverish atmosphere" of a university system that drew "no distinctions, set up no criteria and engaged in every form of miscellanous activity." Flexner doubted whether a mass society could ever be civilized. But, he added, the "American contribution to civilization depends not upon the whole public, but upon a gifted, earnest and agglutinated minority. The minority needs to be protected against the beating waves of mediocrity and humbug."[4]

This must have been music to Nock's ears: perhaps the road back to the humane life was not so long as he imagined. In the same year that Flexner's book appeared, Nock, possibly motivated by a desire to protect the "gifted, earnest and agglutinated minority," accepted a visiting professorship at Bard College. Bard was the new name of his alma mater, which had recently been absorbed by Columbia University but maintained the independent status of a college. Nock was astonished, as were many of his friends, that Columbia would permit Bernard Iddings Bell, Bard's president, to offer the post to "a professed anarchist, individualist and single-taxer." What was more, he was to teach politics and history "on his own terms." Ellery Sedgwick was delighted. He wrote Nock of his amazement at hearing that heathendom's ambassador was now accredited to a Christian college, and speculated on the fun Nock's students would have as they followed him through Jefferson, Guillaume Du Bellay, Rabelais, and Artemus Ward. Sedgwick was glad the appointment would keep his friend in America, but warned Nock that the outrages he would encounter would sandpaper his soul.[5]

For the first few months Nock was enthusiastic about the "experiment." He was pleased with his students and with the academic freedom that prevailed. He was also delighted to be able to "hand out the Word with the bark on it" and not be run out of town. The "word," judging by his correspondence, was a blistering critique of the woolly-minded and sentimental distortions of reality by democratic theory. By spring he had prepared a series of lectures for the University of Virginia. His Page-Barbour lectures were subsequently published in a small but influential book, *The Theory of Education in the United States*. By the time of their publication Nock had, judiciously, fled the academic scene.[6]

Abraham Flexner, whose book Nock had obviously read, had begun his exposé by quoting Lord Haldane: "It is in universities . . . that the soul of a people mirrors itself." Nock had no quarrel with this observation, nor was he in substantial disagreement with Flexner's description of the universities. But Nock was intent on showing what the shallow misconceptions of pseudodemocratic theory had led to.[7]

In *The Theory of Education in the United States* Nock repeated most of his earlier strictures against popular public education. Then he set about to explain the deeper causes of its failure. In his view, careless use of language had led to misunderstanding of equality and democracy and of the value of literacy. Faulty, misconceived democratic principles had been turned into absolutes. *Equality*, for example, had come to mean in practice the "rabid self-assertion . . . of ignorance and vulgarity." Democracy, as popularly understood, encouraged a "strong resentment of superiority. It resents the thought of an élite." The idea, Nock wrote, that there exist "ranges of intellectual and spiritual experience, achievement and enjoyment, which by nature are open to some and not to all" was repugnant to pseudo-equalitarian democratic dogma. On the contrary, according to the prevailing conception of democracy, "in the realm of the spirit everybody is able to enjoy everything that anybody can enjoy, so the popular idea of democracy postulates that there shall be nothing worth enjoying . . . that everybody may not enjoy." The benighted spirits who were skeptical of such aggressive demands for mediocrity were exposed to all "the evils of a dogged, unintelligent, invincibly suspicious resentment." Thus, Nock lamented, there must be "no ideals above those of the average man."[8]

To complete the perverted triad of contemporary democratic dogma, Nock turned to the supposition that a literate public insures honest government and vigilant public opinion—presumably the *raison d'être* of public education. He thought this a blind spot in Jefferson, who had proposed the outlandish notion in the face of all the evidence of reason and experience. Merely to be able to make one's way over a printed page without grasping more than the elemental ideas was hardly, Nock scoffed, a means to informed opinion. The contrary was true: the mass mind because of its literacy was ripe for manipulation by every rogue, demagogue, and huckster. In an *Atlantic* article he continued this argument, maintaining that in Portugal, with its notoriously high rate of illiteracy, the people were better off. The countryside was not marred by advertisements, and literature of genuine merit had a far higher circulation than in America. Lisbon, he claimed, was noted for some of the world's finest bookstores, uncluttered with popular trash and other trivia. His travels confirmed the judgment of a French authority that the country encouraged a small elite group, extremely brilliant and well-read.[9]

Nock contrasted this cultural tradition with that in America, where an aspiring elite had been so harassed that it became almost nonexistent. In America there was a high rate of literacy. As a consequence, "immense masses of garbage" were daily shot from the presses. Where, Nock asked, was the gain to civilization? From observing life in America and in Portugal, where he had viewed the contentment of worker and peasant through a perspective that shaped the world as he wished it to be, he developed a somewhat perverse application of Gresham's law: by encouraging the production of poor literature, mass literature drives out the good and lowers civilized standards. Gresham's law may not apply here because, according to it, people circulate bad currency in order to preserve the good, whereas in Nock's application the people preserve bad literature because they prefer it to good. But perhaps in Nock's view there was no fallacy. Gresham's law implied some wisdom and discrimination by the masses. Nock, however, had concluded that the vast majority of men were uneducable and their pursuit of the shoddy and vulgar therefore inevitable. Given this premise, his application of Gresham was logical. He echoed the views of an earlier skeptic of democratic culture, E. L. Godkin, who before the turn of the century had warned that "ignorance, so far as it is vested with power, tends to drive out intelligence just as debased currency tends to drive out gold."[10]

In less than a decade Nock had come a long way from his perfectionist declarations in the *Freeman*. He no longer attributed the deplorable state of American culture to the injustices of an exploitative economic system; at least, this was no longer his major premise. Now, quite frankly accepting Mencken's charges, he denied the innate potential of most men to benefit by education. Popular democratic theory had proved wanting because it postulated a populace that was educable, whereas "relatively very few are educable, very few indeed." Nock disclosed that the "vast majority of mankind" had "neither the force of intellect to apprehend the processes of education, nor the force of character to make an educational discipline prevail in their lives." Since most men are "structurally immature," no amount of exposure to instruction or example could ever "determine in them the demands of life that are characteristic of maturity."[11]

Nock owned that even the most minimal intelligence could respond to some kind of training, but that had nothing to do with education. It was time to recognize the fact and abandon the absurd pretense of calling training schools colleges and universities. Americans, Nock charged, establish so-called educational institutions, load them "to the gunwales with ineducable persons, proceed to train them in bricklaying, dish-washing, retail shoe-merchandising, or what not, and then insist that there should be somewhere a poor pennyworth of bread thrown in with this intolerable deal of sack." Nock did not agree with Flexner on the possibility of a compromise whereby colleges and universities might continue their vocational-training programs and still offer educational opportunities. "How is it possible," he asked, "really, as a matter of what old-school psychologists called 'the common sense of mankind,' for an institution to affirm a pseudo-equalitarian, pseudo-democratic theory at one end of its campus, and deny it at the other?"[12]

Although Nock was critical of "progressive educators," the major assumption of his book confirmed their view that "training for life," "life adjustment," and child-centered education justified watering down curricula because of low intelligence and the democratic necessity of educating everyone. Arthur Bestor, a zealous and persuasive surveyor of the "educational wastelands," has shown that much progressive educational theory, when stripped of euphemism and sentimentality, rested on the premise that as many as 60 per cent of all school-age youngsters were not equipped for academic instruction or vocational training; "life adjustment" was to be their fate. According to Bestor, the progressive educators were really saying that the majority would remain hewers of wood and drawers of water. Paradoxically, in the name of equalitarian democracy, the theory of traditional elitism was revived.[13]

Perhaps even more quixotic was Nock's apparent readiness to invoke the authority of science. His book in part reflected the contemporary New Humanist skepticism of science and reaffirmation of man's spiritual, transcendent nature, which lay beyond scientific investigation. Although Nock disdained the popular awe of science, he was quick to accept for his own purposes the dubious intelligence measurements advanced by educational psychologists and given particular prominence because of the intelligence tests that the army administered to draftees during World War I. The results of the tests, as interpreted by their designers, led to the assumptions that mental ages were fixed and that a vast number of American adults had the mental capacity of fourteen-year-old children. Many progressive educators seized on the information to justify their theories. Richard Hofstadter has found this phenomenon one of the more perplexing features of the progressive education movement. Because of it, in the name of progress a large number of American youths were written off as uneducable.[14]

Nock used the tests to buttress his developing elitism. Like many disciples of educational testing, he, too, ignored the intellectual, cultural, and environmental factors in intelligence. His views were remarkably like those of Edward Lee Thorndike, who had played a leading part in standardizing and applying the army tests. Thorndike, never an advocate of educational equality, believed that heredity was far more important than environment in determining intelligence, which was the product of an individual's innate characteristics. He was convinced that academic study was beyond most students.[15]

Membership in the saving Remnant, then, was determined by the mysterious, almost Calvinistic, influence of heredity. Some were gratuitously chosen to be endowed with intelligence, and most were not. The chosen few, theoretically at least, might appear in any society and come from any environment. The crucial problem of education was to devise a method of protecting this Remnant.

The first step, Nock said, was to recognize quite frankly that American institutions of higher learning were at best training centers rather than educational institutions, and to stop calling them colleges and universities. "Precision in nomenclature" was an initial step toward intellectual integrity: "One can easily cheat oneself with words; one can as easily intoxicate oneself with them." There still remained the problem of the educable person. As matters stood, his talents, once thought useful in a civilized society, simply went to waste. Every effort was expended on the motor-minded, while society continued to ignore the educable Remnant. To continue in this manner would be to court disaster.[16]

Nock, however, did not hold out much hope that it would be averted. He frequently returned to the example of medieval universities, where wandering scholars sought out great teachers and dedicated their lives to studying the best that had been thought and said in the world. These scholars and teachers had been true citizens of the glorious "Republic of Letters." Even as late as 1900, Nock felt, he could have named a few members of that republic in America's colleges and universities. But since then the technicians, experts, manipulators, and organizers had taken over. He playfully entertained the idea of persuading a private philanthropy to establish a set of institutions designed to serve the educable elite and "consecrated to an unswerving service of the Great Tradition." It would consist of a secondary school, an undergraduate college, and a university containing only the four traditional faculties of law, literature, theology, and medicine. Such a university would have to wait a long time for eligible students, but if it held out against "all the force of wind and tide," it would eventually attract the educable. He recognized the project as no more than a dream, however, since there was no possibility of recruiting a faculty. In America the art of knowing how to be "on living terms with the Great Tradition" had been lost.[17]

For all Nock's inability to propose any alternative except a return to the aristocratic view of knowledge as the contemplation of fixed verities, one cannot disregard his sad description of the failure of popular education. The testimony of more detached scholars supports many of his observations. As a critic of the sentimentality and hypocrisy that had become dominant within the educational hierarchy, he was both articulate and persuasive. His criticism anticipated that of a later generation, which, perhaps for quite different reasons, has also discovered the problems inherent in genuinely educating a mass society. In his recent indictment of public "compulsory mis-education," another anarchoindividualist, Paul Goodman, raises many of the same points as Nock and in some cases comes to similar conclusions. Certainly Goodman's observation that most students should not be in a scholastic setting and that their compelled presence "causes dilution and stupefying standardization" is consistent with Nock's foreboding; and his charge that contemporary college administrators and faculty have at best a "tenuous loyalty to the culture of the Western world, the Republic of Letters" and have transformed the university into "nothing but a factory to train apprentices and process academic union-cards" could have been written by Nock.[18]

However, the similarity between Nock and Goodman ends with the conditions they describe. Goodman is closer to the earlier Nock who spoke up eloquently for anarchist perfectionism and directed his criticism primarily at an exploitative economic and social system. *The Theory of Education in the United States* marked an important turning point in Nock's career. His former humanitarian anarchism had become elitist. Despite the book's penetrating observations, sharp witticisms, and occasional good humor, it was written in despair and frustration. In 1914 he had strongly endorsed progressive education as promoted by William Wirt in the Gary school system and, earlier in the century, had championed it as an opportunity given immigrants and underprivileged persons to prove themselves eager for and capable of education. But now he found the idea of popular education a chimera. As for the great tradition of the republic of letters, that would never return to America. It might endure in other parts of the world but was totally superfluous in American society. Lord Haldane was right: the educational system does mirror the soul of a nation, and America's soul was beyond redemption.

In 1935 Nock confided in his journal that of late he had acquired a reputation for being a "senile Tory," whereas twenty years earlier he had been regarded as a "violent radical." But although he frequently insisted that in America too much effort was being expended on the "prolotoorios," he denied that he had abandoned any fundamental conviction. He was still, he argued, for justice. "Up to four years ago," Nock wrote in his journal, "I was an anarchist. I thought, and still think, that if one accept the doctrine that human nature will in the long run show itself capable of indefinite improvement, the only logical social philosophy is that of anarchism. . . . Of late, however, my faith in this doctrine has become impaired." Nock added that he had not come to total disbelief but to the point of "serious uncertainty." The elitism on which the anarchist vision often seems to rest came abruptly to the surface with Nock's astonishing discovery of the aristocratic revelations of an architect and misanthropic social critic, Ralph Adams Cram.[19]

Cram is a fascinating, if neglected, figure. He, as much as any other American, carried on the tradition of Henry Adams, a tradition that did not mellow with time. Indeed, he was responsible for the first publication of *Mont-Saint-Michel and Chartres*. As a young student of architecture in Rome, Cram had been converted from "the ethical culture and the respectable deism of the 'liberal' Protestant denominations" to the Episcopal church. His conversion had been motivated by aesthetic dedication to the form of medieval architecture, but it developed into a profound commitment to the theological tenets of Catholicism as the only way of maintaining an ordered and intelligible world.[20]

Cram became a successful leader of the neo-Gothic revival in America. His work was commissioned by Yale and Princeton universities and by countless churches. But Cram was much more than an architect. His profession, as he understood it, was a quest for the eternal elements of excellence and beauty: no matter what the medium, art was never an individual response to stimuli, but was rather the expression of the best in any time or place. Beauty was not in the eye of the beholder but was an entity in itself, immutable and everlasting. The study and practice of architecture Cram believed to be the best means of searching out beauty, for it went "deep down into the social fundament . . . it meant isolating the best from the general ruck." For Cram, architecture was the physical embodiment of a social and cultural ideal of order, form, and discrimination. In his writing on architecture there is a similarity to Nock's writing on the Remnant. Cram loved the Gothic cathedrals of France because their monumental spires rose out of the general mediocrity of their surroundings, symbolizing Christ, who rose above the rabble from humble beginnings as an example to mankind.[21]

In 1917, when war and bloodshed reigned in Europe, Cram wrote *The Nemesis of Mediocrity* to explain why the world had come on evil times. His statement that true democracy was the "noblest idea ever discovered by man or revealed to him" is seldom quoted by critics or admirers. True democracy meant three things: abolition of privilege, equal opportunity for all, and utilization of ability—ideals that had never been achieved because democracy as practiced made their achievement impossible. In the name of democracy the "valleys are being filled in and the mountains brought low"—all merit and beauty and excellence reduced to a colorless, uniform mediocrity.[22]

As Cram saw it, mankind was being reduced to a uniformly low level incapable of producing or even wanting leadership. Mass society only accepted leaders who conformed to its limited aspirations. A society "without the supreme leadership of men who by nature or divine direction can speak and act with and by authority" was, Cram warned, a far greater menace to civilization than autocracy. In the past, men and nations had achieved greatness not by the will of a numerical majority but by the "supreme leadership of the few—seers, prophets, captains of men." Democracy deliberately denied distinction in all fields, except possibly business, which fostered "little men, blinded, puzzled and appalled" by the crisis of modern times, without the stature, the intelligence, or the spiritual strength to lead the way out of the wilderness; " 'Mene, Tekel, Upharsin' is on the wall in words of fire and blood, and the Belshazzars of modernism can neither understand them, nor, which is worse, find their interpreter, therefore they and we go on to our predestined fate."[23]

Cram's jeremiads, moreover, were heavily laced with racism. From Beacon Hill, Cram surveyed the invading immigrant hordes and the polyglot culture they were creating in Boston. His fellow Brahmins had long been leaders in a genteel form of aristocratic nativism, and many had played leading roles in the Immigration Restriction League. If he was not a member of the league, it is almost certain that he enthusiastically supported its work. One of the most frightful aspects of democracy, he asserted, was the breaking down "of the just and normal barriers of race." By "free and reckless mixing of incompatible strains," pure-blood specimens were replaced by mongrels.[24]

Although Cram, like Nock, was critical of the naturalism of the new sciences, he, too, was quick to accept their most dubious theories to support his arguments. Thus he could write that it was a "commonplace of sociology that the American-born son of the foreign-born immigrant of a decadent race or inferior blood who himself had reacted to the stimulus of a new environment and unprecedented educational opportunities, is not in general an advance over his progenitor either in character or capacity. . . ." On the contrary, no matter how great his educational acquirement, he almost invariably proved to be "a retrogression and return to type." This primitive application of Mendelian eugenics convinced Cram that racial intermixture was hazardous for civilization. It seems quite clear that Cram had read carefully Madison Grant's *The Passing of the Great Race*, published a year before his own prophecies. Grant, a man of aristocratic pretensions, had ransacked the work of eugenists and physical anthropologists to buttress his racist dogma. One of his principal articles of faith was that races must never blend because the "mixture of two races gives us a race reverting to the more ancient, generalized and lower type." Following the same line of thought, Cram warned that with the "hybridization of race," already in an advanced stage in much of America and part of Europe, the time was near when the "spiritual factors" of civilization would be negated and the race (he apparently meant descendants of the Anglo-Saxons) would disappear into oblivion.[25]

Ralph Adams Cram had by 1932 become one of America's most disdainful critics of democratic liberalism, so it was natural that he should turn to the welcoming pages of Mencken's *American Mercury*. By the 1930s the good humor that had once characterized Mencken's crusade against the booboisie had turned sour and even malicious. The magazine, shrill with tirades against democracy, offered a platform to a growing number of alienated prophets of doom. Cram contributed to the journalistic wailing wall an article, "Why We Do Not Behave like Human Beings," which was to have a strong influence on all of Nock's subsequent thought.

Cram wasted no time in explaining his title: most men did not behave like human beings simply because they were not human. By any reasonable standard they were barbarians suffering from delusions of grandeur and could be traced directly back to Neolithic times. The doctrines of evolution and progress were intellectual deceptions, which, like Protestantism, the Reformation, and democracy, had contributed to the calamities of the last millennium. Men had foolishly come to believe that late stages of human development were always superior to early stages, but, Cram wrote, any objective study of mankind showed that this was not the case. Men had, of course, improved certain proficiencies, certain camouflages and mechanistic trappings, but man himself had not undergone any essential change. If one judged mankind by the character, capacity, and achievement of outstanding individuals, man stood as high five thousand years ago as he had at any time since. A few distinguished human beings had always risen above the undifferentiated mass.[26]

Cram's major argument was that scientists, particularly anthropologists, had erred in categorizing the undifferentiated mass as human, for the distinction between the savage mob and those who were a glory to the human race was infinitely greater than that between anthropoid apes and the mob. Therefore, he said, the line of demarcation should be drawn not between primitive man and the ape but between a glorified human being and the Neolithic mass. In Cram's view the Neolithic mass constituted the raw material from which occasional human beings emerged. Not Darwin but de Vries was right when he asserted that evolution occurred not from "lower to higher and by the constant accretion of minute differences, but by . . . the catastrophic process: the periodical and unaccountable appearance, in the midst of many type forms, of one that is entirely new." Cram compared the Neolithic mass to an eternal stream of molten lava. Occasionally it fountained in fine personalities—"slim jets of golden lava, that caught the sun and opened into delicate fireworks of falling jewels, beautiful beyond imagination"—and from these fountains alone could men establish genuine criteria for humanity.

According to Cram, great human beings appear from time to time, who, endowed with inventive talent and enormous energy, create whatever is civilized. But inevitably they are overwhelmed by barbarian mediocrity. Modernism's perverse and misleading doctrines of popular education, democratic government, equalitarianism, and universal suffrage, as well as the unlimited opportunities of industrial civilization, may have clothed modern mass man in deceptive garments, but underneath he was still a primitive barbarian indistinguishable from his Neolithic ancestors. Predictably, the Renaissance, Reformation, Enlightenment, and French Revolution were all described by Cram as consequences of the grand delusion that had led modern man to his *Götterdämmerung*: "Political and social democracy, with their plausible devices and panaceas; popular sovereignty, the Protestant religion of the masses; the technological triumphs that were to emancipate labor and redeem the world; all the multiple manifestations of a free and democratic society" had failed of their predicted issue. The persistence of the "everlasting Neolithic Man and his assumption of universal control" explained the comprehensive failure and the impossibility of recovery.[27]

On 10 September 1932 Nock recorded in his journal, almost simultaneously with the publication of Cram's article, his discovery that there was something wrong with the zoological classification of human beings: "Not everyone who answers to *homo sapiens* is human; relatively few are." Scientists, he added, did not test their criteria for humanity against the best products of human nature. "There is," he wrote, in what is almost a crib from Cram, "a greater difference between Socrates, Marcus Aurelius, Sophocles, and the man of the crowd, than there is between the man of the crowd and the higher anthropoids."[28]

And so the aristocratic elitist and the self-proclaimed philosophical anarchist joined forces against mass culture. It is one of the ironies of history that the masses, a euphemism for other people, invariably become the scapegoat for the alienated, reactionary or revolutionary. Fear and distrust of the masses can be found in every political sector. A conservative is chagrined that millions no longer pay deference to an elite. A liberal, dismayed by his failure to re-create the world in his image and seeking ways to sidestep the inefficiences of democratic process, becomes defensive about the people's misuse of their educational and political opportunities. And a revolutionary, disgruntled by the bourgeois aspirations of the "revolutionary" masses, concludes that their natural, working-class consciousness has been transformed into sheeplike apathy and debilitating acquiescence. As the socialist Michael Harrington recently put it: "Who is destroying Western culture? One of the most ubiquitous answers of the century was and is: the masses."[29]

Soon Nock was to join the plaintive chorus of this exhausted elite. His journal indicates that he had toyed with ideas like Cram's for some time. Two books had particularly aroused his interest. The first, *Immortability: An Old Man's Conclusions*, was written by the Reverend Samuel David McConnell, an Episcopal minister and church historian. The title alone captured the nostalgia and premonition of decadence that attracted an increasing audience during the period between the wars. McConnell, who was eighty-five, sought through a synthesis of psychology, cultural anthropology, and theology to affirm a transcendent, spiritual immortality for the few whom he called "psychic human beings." His rejection of the scientific classification of the human species was what interested Nock. After observing the crowds that inhabited American cities, with shallow lives, brutal existence and, at best, cunning intelligence, McConnell questioned whether they were really human. They did not appear to be men endowed with a "psychic existence" and an "awareness that life is more than just living." Men who were so endowed stood out from the mass and had qualities that were not propagated merely by reproduction. McConnell charged that scientific measurement ignored psychic existence, which was the true mark of humanity. Nock showed little interest in McConnell's speculations on immortality, but was alive to his observations supporting the ideas of Cram.[30]

The second book that impressed Nock was Ortega y Gasset's *Revolt of the Masses*, an English translation of which was published in 1932. It gave the developing tradition of despair a popular slogan. To describe Ortega as an authoritarian opponent of liberal democracy would be an oversimplification, though he severely criticized its historical performance. What he feared most was that the "select few" talented men in Western society were losing their rightful, necessary positions of influence and being overwhelmed by spontaneous mass movements, which would lead to a dictatorial tyranny of either the right or left. Ortega's influential book began with the assertion that the single fact of greatest importance to the Western world was the "accession of the masses to complete social power." Since it was obvious to all thinking men that the masses neither could nor should direct even their own lives, their assumption of supremacy confronted modern civilization with a crisis. Although Ortega, like Cram, described mass men as primitive, comparing them to the "perennially primitive [whom] Breyssig has called . . . 'the peoples of perpetual dawn,' " the essence of his argument was that mass man, not arrogant but pathetic, was the most disastrous product of the modern world.

Ortega likened the mass man to a "spoiled child" born to wealth and luxury who had no notion of the creative energy and imagination that had been exerted to provide him with the conveniences he took for granted. Quite correctly believing himself commonplace, mass man refused to make any demands on himself; this distinguished him from exceptional human beings. Nevertheless, in spite or because of his fatuous existence, mass man demanded that everyone should be like himself. With his great awe of machinery, he had become a victim of the greatest machine of all—the state, a gigantic, interlocking bureaucracy oppressive to all individuality and spontaneity. "What will be left in the end?" asked Ortega, and he answered: "A bloodless skeleton, dead with that rusty death of machinery, more gruesome than the death of a living organism."[31]

Nock joined these Cassandras in January 1933 with a *Harper's Magazine* article entitled "Are All Men Human?" A rationale for elitist withdrawal and resignation, it began with a brief survey of the ideas of Cram, McConnell, and Ortega. Then Nock turned to what he believed to be the logical implications of their observations. If, he wrote, one entertained Cram's view that most members of the human race were, in fact, poor brutes, then that was the obvious explanation for the anomalies that had perplexed reflective men for centuries. For example, why had men behaved like "maddened apes"? Because they were maddened apes. If men acted, in the words of Carlyle, like "tamed vipers" in an Egyptian pitcher, "each struggling to get its head above the others," it was because mass men are not human beings but brutes. If one recognized this reality, there was no longer any anomaly in man's behaving as a brute and not as a human being.[32]

There was, Nock continued, a good deal of evidence to support his conclusion. Men showed little grasp of long-range problems because as brutes they could not see beyond an immediate benefit. If a human being was, as McConnell suggested, psychically distinct from brute man, then it was no wonder that mass man was handier at mechanical enterprises than at moral ones. Conversely, if a human being was indeed an exception, one should expect him to be ineffectual in the non-human society that engulfed him. This, Nock commented, "seems always to have been the case, and never more clearly so than now."[33]

If all this was true, then obviously it was absurd to lodge sovereignty in "the people." For that was to assume that the people were human and thus capable of a degree of development competent to self-government. On the other hand, if the people—drawing on Hamilton, not Jefferson—were "a great beast" then the whole philosophy of the Enlightenment was an exercise in futility.[34]

Nock could not let the subject drop. His journal and letters repeatedly referred to Cram's thesis and evidence that he believed supported it. "The Quest of the Missing Link," published in the *Atlantic Monthly,* was a restatement and refinement of the argument he considered important enough to include in a collection of his writings published in 1937. He acclaimed Cram's revelations as a "brand-new idea" about the nature of man and his relation to other forms of life. The implications were so far-reaching that he was dismayed that Cram's initial article and his own elaboration had not caused a stir among anthropologists and psychologists. He assumed that because the articles had appeared in popular magazines they had not come to the attention of serious scholars or had been passed off as "a bit of more or less playfully sensational journalism."[35]

He continued to comment and speculate, for he felt that if Cram's views were taken seriously, as they should be, they would challenge the prevailing ideas of anthropologists, psychologists, political theorists, social philosophers, and theologians. Modern man's entire world view would be subject to drastic revision; his thoughts, feelings, and aspirations could not help being profoundly affected. To illustrate how the revelations of Cram had altered his own perspective, he told how, on leaving his hotel one morning, he had been shocked to see a man scavenging in a garbage pail. It had made a painful impression on him. However, he had soon come across a stray dog doing the same thing and had not been at all distressed, for he had felt that the dog had been living up to its innate potentialities while the man had not. But, aided by Cram's understanding, Nock had grasped his error in perspective: "I was governed by the presumption that the man was a human being." He acknowledged that that might have been the case, for Cram had conceded that occasionally even a human being lived in poverty and neglect. Nevertheless, the probabilities were strongly that the man was not psychically human. "Well, then," concluded Nock, "if Mr. Cram is right, one's feeling for the man would obviously change."[36]

After this misanthropic parable Nock turned on his former idols Henry George and Thomas Jefferson. George, in whom the "perfectionist doctrine . . . served as his only spring of action," had been completely deluded. As for Jefferson, Nock found his naïve faith in popular sovereignty and the principles of republicanism absurd. Nock had marveled at how long it had taken him to understand the true nature of the average man. He had taken his faith from Jefferson for years, but now, he saw, "Jefferson was curiously inconsistent. When he spoke from instinct or experience, he would say things like 'What a bedlamite is man!' When he spoke from theory, he over-rated the average man; his faith in him seems to have been the pure outshot of political theory." The virtue of Nock's new understanding, derived from Cram, was that it did not rest on abstract theorizing and hopeful abstractions. It was grounded in common-sense observation and experience.[37]

Under the general, all-embracing label of republicanism, Nock argued, could be found the root of all the evils of the modern world. Republicanism had created the modern state and made it a "pliant organ of such segments of the Neolithic mass as can get at it, one after another, and work it for their own behoof." The record of republicanism bore witness to little that was human in the Neolithic mass. It encouraged a two-way system of corruption. The mass corrupted the state, and the state still further corrupted the mass, bringing about conditions "increasingly repulsive and degrading."[38]

Nock was not content with the overriding generalizations of Cram. Since the doctrines of the Enlightenment had proved false and pernicious, they should be replaced by laws that accurately described the follies of mankind. He gradually developed a system of three fundamental laws governing the conduct of mass men, if not that of human beings. The first, his version of Gresham's law, explained the dangers of mass literacy and of all forms of equalitarianism, which, by demanding mediocrity, made excellence obsolete. The second, the law of diminishing returns, disproved the notion that if a few humans benefited from a cultural experience, any number could obtain the same benefit. Numbers were in themselves self-defeating. A few people could attend a chamber concert and come away exhilarated, but if the room were packed with forty or fifty people, the experience would be lost. The implications for mass education and culture were obvious.[39]

The capstone of Nock's system, the third "natural law," was revealed to him inadvertently by Edward Epstean, who, in a vigorous discussion had exclaimed: "I tell you, if self-preservation is the first law of human conduct, exploitation is the second." As a careful student of Henry George, Nock had frequently cited George's observation that "man tends always to satisfy his needs and desires with the least possible exertion." But he had only considered this within the context of George's development of the principle of economic rent. Now he understood its broader application. For if George was right, and Nock was sure that he was, "then certainly exploitation [was] an inescapable corollary, because the easiest way to satisfy one's needs and desires is by exploitation." Indeed, one might say, "Exploitation is the first law of conduct, since even in self-preservation one tends always to take the easiest way."[40]

For Nock all the old contradictions and ambiguities were resolved. In the past he had, in attacking the state, described man's natural instinct to exploit by using political means to expropriate property. At the same time, when upholding the doctrine of philosophical anarchism with its belief in the possibility of human perfection, he had insisted on man's instinctive desire for freedom and its practical objective, "that men may become as good and decent, as elevated and noble, as they might be and really wished to be." Supplementing Cram's theory and the three natural laws, Nock threw over the traces of perfectionism and retained anarchism as a purely elitist doctrine.

This helps to explain how Nock could accept Cram's argument that self-improvement by the mass man was impossible and, at the same time, reject Cram's call for some form of elitist authoritarianism. In Nock's view, authoritarianism was as ineffective as equalitarianism; also, the establishment of a "human oligarchy" composed of an enlightened Remnant was quite hopeless because the political ascendancy of the mass had reached the point at which it could not be checked. All one could do was to keep out of the way, "like a man sheltering himself behind a wall against a hurricane," and cultivate one's virtues while waiting quietly for the inevitable end.[41]

Nock persistently rejected the logical authoritarianism explicit in Cram's argument in an attempt to preserve a vestige of his professed anarchism. It was clear to him that if one accepted Cram's entire argument, "it would enforce a radical change upon one's whole social outlook. Philosophical anarchism, with its profound belief in the essential goodness of *Homo sapiens*, becomes less than tenable; it becomes grotesque." This was true if one made no distinction between the mass of men and the few superior human beings. But an elitist, rather than a philosophical, anarchism, stripped of its humanistic rhetoric, offered Nock justification for his insistence on the right of absolute freedom for noble men. It seems clear that his enthusiastic acceptance of Cram's misanthropic ideas allowed him finally to express the elitism that had long been a submerged but fundamental aspect of his anarchism. He had believed in Matthew Arnold's idea of the Remnant but had apparently never really accepted Arnold's mildly democratic faith that the Remnant would eventually expand to constitute the entire society. As Lionel Trilling has pointed out, Arnold had "the democratic insight that a human value exists in the degree that it is shared . . . that a good may have meaning but no reality until it is participated in. . . ." It is true that Nock, while editor of the *Freeman*, had voiced this missionary obligation. However, the elitist inclinations in his personality had always been strong; but with the help of Cram they prevailed.[42]

It would be a mistake to make light of Nock's acceptance of Cram's ideas. On the contrary, his discipleship approached the dimensions of a religious conversion. During the remainder of his life Nock seldom wrote an article on politics, culture, or social organization in which he did not try to apply Cram's dogma and refer to Cram's "brilliant thesis." Nearly a decade after his first reading of Cram he wrote Paul Palmer, who was editor of the *American Mercury*, that his understanding of Cram was the most valuable legacy he could leave the younger man. He devoted pages in his *Memoirs* to his initial discovery of Cram and its profound effect on all his thought. He recalled struggling to maintain his Jeffersonian perfectionism as long as possible while trying without success to poke holes in Cram's argument: "Left in the lurch . . . I ended by striking my colours as gracefully as possible, parted company with the theologians, with Mr. Jefferson, with Price, Priestley, Condorcet, Rousseau, Mme. de Staël, and went over to the opposition with head unbowed and withers still unwrung."[43]

Nock no longer walked an intellectual tightrope. He was protected by Cram's revelation from the despondency that gripped many of his contemporaries, who stood forlorn and naked beside the collapsed structure of dogmatic optimism that had sheltered eighteenth- and nineteenth-century thought. In the *Memoirs* he recalled a peculiar and unforeseen consequence of his new vision: the old problem of suffering fools gladly had vanished. He found himself quite unable to hate or even lose patience with anybody: "One can hate human beings, at least I could,—I hated a lot of them when that is what I thought they were,—but one can't hate sub-human creatures or be contemptuous of them, wish them ill, regard them unkindly."

Thus, not by achieving the vision tempered by shrewdness yet unscarred by cynicism but by adopting a calculated misanthropy, Nock achieved the serenity of Rabelaisian superiority. He was sure that he had finally established his role as a detached observer of mankind's follies, analyzing, recording, and describing all he saw for an alien, impotent Remnant. Although he denied feeling even mild contempt for the majority of mankind, his candid, frequently brutal, elitism seemed to illustrate Schopenhauer's observation that "if a man sets out to hate all the miserable creatures he meets he will not have much energy left for anything else; whereas he can despise them one and all with the greatest ease."[44]

7. Anarchist Attentats

NOCK'S ANARCHIST ELITISM, despite his protestations, did not enable him to achieve the detachment he so greatly desired. He had not come to hate, but he was unable to stifle his contempt for, mankind.

In April 1933 he wrote that he was above all "thankful that the Lord's mercy" had permitted him "to live out of America most of the time since 1920 and thus escape contact with its social and economic manias and puerilities." His near-expatriation had encouraged his best work. But the thirties tested his resolve. Hoover's administration was as depressing to Nock as the administrations of Harding and Coolidge. Hoover was reputed to be a rugged individualist, but Nock saw him as a noisome example of materialistic Philistinism, *"Fordismus."* In Nock's view Hoover was never more than a political lackey of the business community, which used the state for its own interests.[1]

If Nock seldom had a kind word for politicians, he was even harsher on businessmen. No one in his right mind could expect principle from a politician, but the hypocrisy and sophistry of businessmen showed how "thoroughly rotten, the whole structure of American business" was and how "utterly flagitious" the principles of the nation's economic life.[2]

Nock never trusted the antistatist claims of industrialists who preached individualism and laissez faire—"imposter-terms," according to Nock. Calling themselves individualists, American businessmen clamored for government aid in the form of subsidies, tariffs, and other forms of state intervention designed for their economic advantage. Professing to abhor collectivism, they urged the state to take up measures that led to it. The Federal Trade Commission, Department of Commerce, Federal Farm Board, and many other regulatory agencies were, Nock charged, examples of business's use of the state. Businessmen might proclaim their love for laissez faire, but "no such régime ever existed in this country; American business never followed a policy of *laissez-faire,* never wished to follow it, never wished the State to let it alone."[3]

Like Herbert Spencer and William Graham Sumner, Nock was a purist who had hoped for an absolute system of laissez faire but no longer expected it to be established. He was astonished, therefore, when friends like Mencken, Amos Pinchot, and Frederic Howe welcomed Franklin Roosevelt's election. To Nock it made no difference who became president; no one could reach the presidency unless he qualified as a machine tender. Roosevelt would be like all the rest—a robot going about the disgusting business of politics—that is, of fleecing the people. Nock didn't vote in 1932; in fact, he couldn't remember when he had last voted. He couldn't even remember the candidates, but he had, he claimed, weighed the issues carefully before casting a write-in vote for Jefferson Davis. "I knew Jeff was dead," he recalled, but voted on the principle that "if we can't have a live man who amounts to anything, by all means let's have a first-class corpse." Nock was certain that that vote had been "as effective as any of the millions" cast since he had voted.[4]

This was pretty much the tone of Nock's correspondence after the 1932 election. From the beginning he had had no respect for Roosevelt, his party, or his program. He scoffed at the claim that Roosevelt had received a mandate from the people. That was "fiddlesticks!—rats!—tripe! A mandate for what? Well, beer; yes, probably beer." Sailing to Brussels in February 1933, before Roosevelt's inauguration in March, he repeated in a journal his appreciation of Catherine Wilson's observation that the skyline of New York was the finest sight in America when viewed from the deck of an outbound steamer.[5]

After six months of the New Deal, Nock was convinced that Roosevelt intended to pursue a policy of "Stateism, pure and simple." Roosevelt had only an electioneering interest in the nation's problems and absolutely no understanding of fundamental economic issues. The New Deal relief and recovery programs reminded Nock of Voltaire's observation that government was a device for taking money out of one man's pocket and putting it into another's.[6]

Like Mencken, whom he now saw frequently, he was particularly irritated by Roosevelt's recruitment of college professors. Nietzsche had been right: "Professors always play the comic rôle in politics."

In Nock's view Roosevelt's advisors constituted "the most extraordinary aggregation of quacks . . . since the death of P. T. Barnum." Relishing the role of critic and social satirist, Nock mixed contempt with sardonic enjoyment of what he considered the more blatant absurdities and delusions of the New Deal reforms, among them all the legislation designed to aid the poor and the unemployed. By adopting the astonishing notion that the state "owes every citizen a living," Roosevelt was transforming "whole batches of men into loafers." Relief recipients, Nock observed, were already so lazy and apathetic that the state's "paternalistic meddling" would soon force Washington "to send janizaries out to follow up 'unemployment relief' and shove food down the unemployed's throats."[7]

Nock seldom seemed aware of the hardship caused by the economic collapse, which was never more than an abstraction to him. He delighted in it as a confirmation of his prediction that the system of grab and exploitation was bound to fail sooner or later. Thus, he could remark that the depression was a good thing, for it would teach the poor to be more self-reliant.[8]

It is hardly surprising that the first organized revolt against the New Deal, the Liberty League, sought Nock's support. He ignored the appeal because he saw little likelihood of disinterested patriotism from the league's promoters, largely disgruntled businessmen. He hoped instead for New Deal opposition that might lead to "something better than *ad captandum* expressions, something a little more intelligent and objective than the dreary run of propagandist outpouring" and the hysteria of the Liberty Leaguers.[9]

Although Nock had engaged in little more than superficial criticism, he wanted to make a serious analysis of what he believed to be the grave dangers facing not only the United States but the entire Western world. He felt that the American political dialogue involved no philosophy, theory, serious study, or speculation, and that it never transcended the partisan, expedient issues of politics. He was dismayed that no American had produced a complete case against the state's progressive usurpation of individual rights. This Nock believed to be the fundamental issue, and yet it was ignored on any profound level by even the progressive opposition to Roosevelt.

Nock repeatedly told his friends that Rooseveltism, Hitlerism, and

Stalinism were all fundamentally the same. There might be differences in degree, but not in kind: all three were "local variants of the common doctrine that man has no natural rights but only such as are created for him by the State."[10] He quoted the German idealists Hegel and Fichte, as well as Mussolini and Lenin, who stressed the state's prerogatives. After reading Alfredo Rocco, the theorist of Italian fascism, Nock informed his friend Bernard Iddings Bell that Rocco's ideas had all been stolen from the German idealist philosophy of the nineteenth century. Where the ideas came from mattered little. The danger was that the state's increasing power would ultimately enslave all citizens. As an anarchist, elitist or not, he was clear as to what constituted bondage: "A man is a slave when his labour-products are appropriated, and his activities are governed, by some agency other than himself; that is the essence of slavery." If political ideologues would refrain from using the words *bolshevism, fascism, Hitlerism, Marxism,* and *communism,* Nock wrote, they would have "no trouble getting acceptance for the principle that underlies them all alike—the principle that the State is everything, and the individual nothing." Anticipating Walter Lippmann's *The Good Society,* published in 1937, Nock described Roosevelt's New Deal as a form of gradual collectivism.[11]

Nock decided that the time was ripe for a full-fledged study of the state and threw himself into the project with an enthusiasm that belied his claim of detachment. He returned to Franz Oppenheimer, Ludwig Gumplowicz, Henry George, and all the others whom he had used as authorities when writing his *Freeman* articles, more than a decade earlier. His new work was spiced with supporting material from Herbert Spencer, Ortega y Gasset, and, of course, Ralph Adams Cram.

The result of Nock's labors was an articulate polemic entitled *Our Enemy, the State.* Nock began by discussing the distinction between the concepts of government and state. He found two historical types of political organization that were mistakenly included under the broad term *government.* As he saw it, a government was a voluntary social organization established by the consent of the governed. A government had purely negative functions; it protected the individual against transgressions encountered in the natural condition of society—fraud, assault, adultery, murder. It was by definition social and existed to meet the legitimate demands of a social community. The state was an altogether different matter. Its origin and function lay in conquest and confiscation. Its interventions, unlike those of government, were invariably positive and undertaken only to facilitate the exploitation of one class or group by another. Its intent and purpose were antisocial.[12]

In his analysis Nock referred to the writings of Paine, Jefferson, Parkman, Spencer, Gumplowicz, and Oppenheimer, but his emphasis was on empirical observation, not theory. Jefferson, for example, had remarked, in *Notes on Virginia*, that certain Indian hunting tribes were "without government." Nock thought Jefferson's terminology misleading; the tribes were without a state but not without government. The same thing could be said with respect to Schoolcraft's observations on the Chippewas and Spencer's on the Bechuanas, Araucanians, and Koranna Hottentots, Nock believed. They were all without "regular" or "definite" governments, but each had an admirable social order to protect the natural rights of the individual members of the tribe. Jefferson had written that the tribes' only controls were their manners and a moral sense of right and wrong. Offenses were punished by tribal contempt and exclusion. Serious crimes were punished by the persons wronged.[13]

It is obvious that Nock's anarchic sentiments had not diminished. He apparently equated the system of manners and mores in primitive societies with a proper, functioning government. It was, in fact, only among a few scattered Indian and African tribes that he could find government, which disappeared as societies became more complex. Again he turned to Marx's premise that the state's development was inevitable only when it was possible to appropriate the land and labor of others. Nock's struggle to distinguish between government and the state is in the tradition of anarchist writing. Enrico Malatesta, for example, dealt with the problem at some length and concluded that the state was "the abstract expression of which the government is the personification." Randolph Bourne, whose *The State* must be included among American anarchist writings, viewed the state similarly, as a concept of power and competition. The government was the machinery by which the state carried out its functions of force and coercion. Both were evil, to Bourne, and he used the word "country" to describe a community of people living in peace and tolerance.[14]

In any case, Nock's recent denigration of mass man made his romanticization of primitive societies irrelevant. If mass man was innately inferior—a savage brute—then the benevolent, co-operative voluntarism of anarchism had no meaning for modern mass society. Nock rejected authoritarianism, but his continued anarchism was negative and nihilistic.

Nevertheless, Nock's purpose was to indict the state from a historical and empirical point of view, although by his own logic the anarchist alternative was now out of the question. He traced the development of American government from its beginnings in England and Holland through the Puritan and colonial periods. What he found was a vast, continuous conspiracy leading to insidious statism. His conclusion, supported by judicious references to Charles Beard, Max Weber, and others, was that a true government based on a genuine democracy had never existed in America. The Puritan political organization had been a merchant-state whose fundamental object had been the exploitation of one class by another; the New England colonists had discovered how the church could be made "a most effective tool of the State."[15]

Nock continued his survey through the revolutionary and constitutional period. The Declaration of Independence may have been the charter of American independence from England, but he believed it to be no barrier against statism. Its principles were quickly abandoned, as an American elite swiftly established the appearance of republicanism without the reality. Nock anticipated recent historical interpretations by scoffing at the supposedly revolutionary character of America's war for independence; it was no more than the overthrow of one state and the establishment of another. Nock, like a later radical anarchist, Paul Goodman, had some sympathy for the government under the Articles of Confederation. At least the use of political means of exploitation had been limited by the fragmentation of power into thirteen nearly autonomous units. Within those autonomies there had been scrambling for privilege but no federal coercive power. Nock, repeating Charles Beard, characterized the establishment of the Constitution as little more than a coup d'état by clever, scheming manipulators, "organized by methods which if employed in any other field than that of politics, would be put down at once as not only daring, but unscrupulous and dishonorable."[16]

Nock continued his anarchist interpretation of American history into the twentieth century. The state, he wrote, ever broadening its power and prestige, through astute use of official monopolies, tariffs, subsidies, and tax programs and by functioning as a manufacturer, educator, insurance salesman, banker, broker, and mail carrier, had spread its all-embracing net over society. In the anarchist tradition, Nock found an example in the government postal monopoly, a service that would be more efficient and cheaper if left to private enterprise. But the state had not assumed such a responsibility without design. The post office was an ever-increasing reservoir for patronage. It was no coincidence that "an administration's chief almoner and whip-at-large" was invariably appointed postmaster general. But the state's most effective tool was its adroit use of republican rhetoric to hide the real purpose of its aggrandizement. Such rhetoric persuaded the citizen that the state was his creation, that state action was his action, and that when the state glorified itself, he was glorified. The greatest single stroke of statist propaganda, Nock wrote, was Lincoln's phrase, "of the people, by the people, for the people."[17]

Armed with the insights of Ortega and Cram, Nock was convinced that modern mass man was peculiarly susceptible to such propaganda. Since he was ignorant of the state's predatory history, he was willing to put "at its disposal an indefinite credit of knavery, mendacity and chicane, upon which its administrators may draw at will." There was no effective opposition since neither major party had any fixed principle or theory beyond the immediate political goal of gaining control of the state's instruments of exploitation. Those out of power called for a return to the Constitution, states' rights, and rugged individualism. Political dialogue in America was mere "agonized fustian."[18]

In Nock's view the New Deal was the latest chapter in a grim drama. Roosevelt had added another function to the state's encroachment on individual rights when he inaugurated the doctrine, new in American history, that the state owes its citizens a living. This Nock judged "an astute proposal for a prodigious enhancement of State power" and an excellent illustration of James Madison's warning against the "old trick of turning every contingency into a resource for accumulating force in the government."[19]

Like his essays in the twenties, *Our Enemy, the State* was concerned with the state's undermining of "social power"—that is, of voluntary, co-operative, community initiative and responsibility. Persons in small, decentralized communities, Nock believed, had once felt a responsibility to others in times of emergency. Now a frequent response was, "Let the State see to it." Ortega's forebodings had become descriptions of reality, Nock saw; the state was after all only a machine, whose existence and maintenance depended on the support of the society on which it fed: "The State, after sucking out the very marrow of society," had already become a mechanical skeleton leading mass man to his fate.[20]

Nock's book captured an immediate if fleeting attention. George Soule, a *New Republic* editor and a leftist critic of the New Deal, surprisingly declared Nock to be one of the "best essayists and soundest commentators on political history" in America. In his judgment Nock's book had managed to "distill more shrewd perception on the Puritan and American revolutions than could be found in any other volume of whatever length." But insofar as Nock's book had a message, Soule, a dedicated exponent of economic planning, could not discover its relevance to the modern world: the author had obviously been since about 1789 in a "cataleptic trance," which had only been interrupted by a brief waking period in which he had read *Progress and Poverty*. Nock also captured the attention and acclaim of the extreme right. Seward Collins, a former Humanist and now a self-proclaimed "fascist" who was editor of the *American Review*, was greatly impressed by the book. It was such a relief, he wrote, "to read a really good book on politics." Nock's "lucidity of thought long ripened in a rich and powerful intellect," had transcended the clouds of smoke put forth by "the Marxian fanatics, the liberal and New Deal sentimentalists, the mess-of-pottage economists . . . the Liberty Leaguers, and old-fashioned Jeffersonian Republicans."[21]

Collins's authoritarian beliefs made him a peculiarly perceptive critic of *Our Enemy, the State*. He was quick to see that it was not, as some suggested, a Jeffersonian document. It was Nock's post-Cram analysis, a repudiation of Jefferson's faith in the potential ability of the average man to govern himself. Collins, enthusiastic in his praise and not put off by Nock's elitist ideas, was sensitive to Nock's pervasive anti-institutionalism, fear of "personal government," and rejection of all authority. Quick to recognize that Nock's analysis was anarchistic, Collins thought that because of its merits within the anarchist genre, it could take a place beside Prince Kropotkin's *Fields, Factories, and Workshops*. Soule's and Collins's judgments—that in spite of Nock's literary and analytical ability the book was irrelevant—supported Nock's contention that the philosophy of statism was the underlying principle of both the right and the left, political labels that were themselves irrelevant and misleading.[22]

It is tempting to describe Nock's *Our Enemy, the State* as another example of what Richard Hofstadter has described as the conspiratorial, "paranoid style" that has often recurred in American intellectual history. Nock's denunciation of such public services as the post office and his assurance that the "principle of absolutism was introduced into the Constitution by the income-tax amendment" are hardly calculated to elicit a sympathetic response from a generation of historians and political scientists whose careers began during the New Deal or post–New Deal era of the welfare state. His anarchic anti-institutionalism seemed increasingly irrelevant and encouraged the image of Nock as a disappointed, nostalgic old man who had simply failed to adjust to the realities of a modern world. Since many liberal historians regard even mild skepticism toward further state centralization as a sign of motivation by self-serving vested interests, by a lingering allegiance to outmoded classical liberalism, or by a regrettable longing for an earlier, less complex age, it is not surprising that Nock has often been judged a member of the hysterical, lunatic-fringe opposition.[23]

There is evidence to support such a judgment. Nock's unrestrained enthusiasm for agrarian primitivism—like that of John Taylor of Caroline, whom he extolled in his book—invited Soule's characterization of Nock as a Rip Van Winkle. Some critics, more favorably disposed toward anarchic views, have noted with chagrin Nock's reliance on Georgite economics. More anachronistic than anarchistic to even so staunch an opponent of the state as Isabel Paterson was Nock's suggestion that the American economy need be no more complex than the bartering of a Yankee rustic "who swaps eggs for bacon in the country store." Such economic fundamentalism, mixed with a romantic attachment to the simple life of tribal or peasant communities, pointed to a strong nostalgia for the past. However, Nock's nostalgia may be compared to the search for simplicity of youthful communal experimenters in the 1960s and 1970s.[24]

Even the symptoms of "paranoid style" in Nock's thought, which grew more obvious during the last few years of his life, are not sufficient cause for dismissing his critique. The convenient, stereotyped historical accusations fall short of the needs of genuine analysis. Nock was seldom in good standing with the conservative right-wingers who opposed the liberal state. Nor can he be placed among the New Humanists, genteel aesthetes whose aristocratic authoritarianism, secular or religious, he consistently rejected. In his speculations and observations there is a serious challenge to support, by liberals, of the centralized state. For all its occasionally extreme rhetoric, his book on the state posed some of the important questions of this century. It takes on a prophetic relevance when a socialist theoretician like R. H. S. Crossman can write: "The planned economy and the centralization of power are no longer socialist objectives. . . . The main task of Socialism today is to prevent the concentration of power in the hands of industrial management or the State bureaucracy—in brief to distribute responsibility and enlarge the freedom of choice." When a moderate liberal scholar like Hans Morganthau can assert that the crisis of contemporary democracy can be attributed to three factors, "the shift of effective material power from the people to the government, the shift of effective power of decision from the people to the government, and the ability of the government to destroy its citizens in the process of defending them," it becomes more difficult to dismiss Nock as superfluous.[25]

Nock's strongest point was his repudiation of the liberal notion that the state had finally become representative of the people. He ridiculed the faith of liberals in the efficacy of popular elections, which he considered a device used by the minority to obtain majority support. He anticipated later leftist criticism of the liberal welfare state, that the very interests that were to be curbed by regulatory legislation had, in fact, gained most by the state's intervention.[26]

Long before Louis Hartz, Daniel Boorstin, and Daniel Bell described and applauded the anti-ideological character of American political dialogue, Nock castigated the New Dealers and their supporters for lacking a political philosophy. The American, he charged, was the "most unphilosophical of beings. . . . He is indifferent to the theory of things." He likened the American people to an army on the march—"a creature of the moment." In his sustained attack on liberals who, in his judgment, supported the state without discrimination, he said that their support or acquiescence was the result of their dislike for ideas. They were mere technicians, expert at tending the state's machinery without purpose or thought beyond the demands of the moment. "Immediatism" was his name for such expedient pragmatism.[27]

What historians have interpreted as political realism and admirable flexibility Nock saw as political expediency and opportunism. In recent years younger historians have pointed to the contradictions and ambiguities of American reform and expressed skepticism about its approach. They have recognized that the New Deal, for example, did not bring about a substantial redistribution of wealth, aid the desperately poor, or provide the stability and security for which it was so long acclaimed. Nock's criticism, negative as it may have been and prompted by other motivations, nevertheless pointed out many of these failures when they were being made.

Nock saw the New Deal as little more than an effort to bolster the status quo. Again anticipating later critics, he warned that increased federal power discouraged local, spontaneous action by individuals and communities. An organized welfare state might provide material comforts and security for a growing middle class, he wrote, but it would not create a society of independent persons shaping their own lives through individual initiative and voluntary community action. Reflective Americans, seeing the awesome power of the state in the latter half of the twentieth century, may agree with Nock, whether they are conservative, liberal, reactionary, or radical.

But Nock's insights were inseparable from the sterility of his anarchic elitism. It was an integral part of his proposition that little patience or understanding would be given to his unorthodox views. Contrary to a recent admirer's assertion, Nock entertained no hope that his work would "point the way for the men of action." On the contrary, in *Our Enemy, the State* he predicted that no one's political opinions were likely to be changed. It was the book's hypothesis, he said, that nothing could be done to change the course of events. One of the characteristic aspects of paranoid thought, according to Hofstadter, is that there is seldom any hope that the evidence presented will convince a hostile world, but the effort to amass it "has the quality of a defensive act which shuts off [the paranoid spokesman's] receptive apparatus and protects him from having to attend to disturbing considerations that do not fortify his ideas. He has all the evidence he needs; he is not a receiver, he is a transmitter."[28]

Nock's argument has all the earmarks of that defensive quality. His purpose was not only to present an anarchist indictment of the state but also to defend his misanthropic elitism. Thus it was imperative for him to present himself as a superfluous man, the victim of a hostile world. His victimization, evidenced by the majority's rejection of his insight, constituted his credentials as an elite spokesman for the Remnant.

Nock elaborated on his self-appointed role in an *Atlantic Monthly* essay, "Isaiah's Job." Except for his articles extolling Cram, it was his most explicit expression of his elitist position. There was, Nock assured his readers, regardless of evidence to the contrary, a Remnant—intelligent human beings, who, while outwardly conforming to the requirements of mass civilization, still respected the plain, intelligent law of things. They were distinct from the "knavish, arrogant, grasping, dissipated, unprincipled, unscrupulous" majority. Nock felt that it was his job, as it had been Isaiah's, to communicate with the "saving Remnant." It was impossible to tell who the members of the Remnant were, where they were, how many there were, or even what they were doing or would do. But it was certain that they existed and that they inevitably found a spokesman. To take on Isaiah's job was particularly important "when everything had gone completely to the dogs," because only from the Remnant could a new society be built. The Remnant needed "to be encouraged and braced up." A book like *Our Enemy, the State* was undertaken merely to edify the Remnant, as part of "Isaiah's job" of keeping the record straight. Thus, careful rationalization affirmed that the very rejection of Nock's views by the majority attested to his superior wisdom.[29]

Ralph Hayes wrote Newton Baker, an older progressive who had become an admirer of Nock, to question Nock's conception of the Remnant as "a single homogeneous thing." It seemed to Hayes that there were an infinite number of Remnants pointing in every direction. He was also skeptical about the Remnant's superiority. Weren't many of its members intolerant of racial nonconformity? Was there any evidence that they were less greedy than the masses? Were they less given to snobbery and provincialism? Hayes doubted that there was, as Nock seemed to suggest, any "beneficence in the mere fact of being out-numbered."[30]

Hayes had put his finger on one of the main flaws in Nock's elitism. Its anarchic anti-institutionalism inevitably threw Nock into the company of a variety of outnumbered dissidents, whom even Nock could hardly have described as members of a "substratum of right thinking and well-doing" human beings. When Nock's old friends and former liberals abandoned individualism to serve the state, he would observe bitterly that the old adage "Politics makes strange bedfellows" was wrong; on the contrary, politics makes the "most natural bedfellowships in the world. Crook lies down with crook in any bed that interest offers; swine snoozes with swine on the litter of any pen that interest opens." However, Nock's astonishing associations in the late thirties and forties laid him open to similar charges.[31]

Not long after Nock began to criticize Roosevelt and the New Deal, he began to hear from leaders of the disorganized opposition. Dorothy Thompson asked if he would meet with Hoover and others interested in the restoration of liberal government. Nock was amused, for he had been astonished by Hoover's bitter polemic against the New Deal, *The Challenge to Liberty:* "Think of such a book on such a subject, by such a man!" he had written. When Nock had published *Our Enemy, the State,* he had wondered "how many people . . . would read a treatise on liberty, written by a disinterested hand." Forgetting that the Lord had told Isaiah that it was impossible to discover who the Remnant were, Nock apparently came to feel that acceptance of his book was a sign of membership in the Remnant and to consider seeking out businessmen who had praised the work. Although he had spent a good part of his career railing at self-seeking business interests, he now had "four or five such folk to see." He still claimed to be "a radical single taxer"—a program that had begun to appeal to conservative businessmen faced with the threat of greater social legislation. Were they, then, and Hoover, too, members of the Remnant?[32]

Nock's anarchist elitism attracted other unlikely associates, the frustrated, Anglo-Saxon, well-to-do Roosevelt haters who welcomed support from any quarter. Neither they nor the "right-thinking" businessmen could be a part of his Remnant, yet slowly he was abandoning all objectivity and aligning himself with them against a common enemy.

Digby Baltzell, a sociologist, and historians of the New Deal have observed that upper-class antipathy to the Roosevelt administration went beyond disagreement with his economic and political programs. Many were obsessed by an "irrational fear, if not horror, of social and racial equality," which seemed to them the ultimate, disastrous consequence of New Deal reform. Roosevelt was held in contempt because he had betrayed his class by refusing to recognize its members as superior people who by right of family, education, and tradition deserved a privileged place in society. The New Deal threatened their caste status and thus drove many to a degree of hysterical hatred and slander that still seems shocking. It is little wonder that these status-conscious patricians should take comfort in Nock's repeated references to the uneducable, brutish masses who were not only being catered to but were gaining the upper hand in society. Despite Nock's frequent disdain for the moneyed class, his ideas expressed their feelings. Nowhere may this be seen more explicitly and in a more damaging way than in his frequent comments on Hitler and the Jews and other immigrant minority groups.[33]

It must be recalled that Nock repeatedly insisted that fascism, communism, Stalinism, and New Dealism were all variants of the same menace—statism. He expressed passionate concern for the fate of the individual in America if the trend toward centralized government continued. However, from the very beginning his response to the rise of Hitler and Nazi Germany was lackluster. He distrusted as liberal propaganda all stories coming out of Germany, preferring to withhold judgment until he had heard the side of a Junker or perhaps "a Hitlerite or two"; he couldn't help "seeing something on the other side." As the evidence of brutal racism piled up, his tone became apologetic; criticism of Nazism would only strengthen Roosevelt and allow him to divert attention from the deplorable failures of the New Deal. After thinking over Hitler's ends, Nock concluded that the Nazis could never have carried their policy through without anti-Semitism. The Jews had defrauded the Weimar Republic of their taxes, and they favored a managed state because they were "the only people who are able to do well out of a managed currency and a fluctuating exchange." Nock had reservations about Hitler, but believed that "the leadership of a wretched lunatic was preferable in the circumstances to none at all."[34]

Nock laced his private journals with derogatory references to Jews. Other persecuted peoples, he wrote, among them the Dutch, Belgians, and Quakers, had gained "some sort of valuable discipline out of persecution, while apparently all that the Jew has got out of it is his vast aptitude for persistence." They had erected the "plea of persecution into a kind of charter," so that if apprehended for a breach of conduct, they would invariably enter a plea of persecution; never suspecting that they might be simply *"ad hoc* objectionable." Nock objected to working in public libraries because they were "infested with Jews, Turks, infidels and heretics." He was angered by a critical letter signed Finkelbein or Finkelstein. He noted in his journal that such letters were "almost invariably signed with names that suggest a very short acquaintance with America" and were "couched in terms that betray an acquaintance with the English language that is even shorter." Their only merit was their "new point of view on America as the land of opportunity." Obviously, these correspondents were not members of Nock's Remnant.[35]

In 1941 Nock wrote a two-part article on "The Jewish Problem in America" for the *Atlantic Monthly.* Subtle and restrained, it was nevertheless a proposal for apartheid for the Jews on the ground that they were Orientals at heart and therefore alien to America's Occidental culture. The Oriental and Occidental, Nock claimed, were incapable of understanding one another. They might live side by side and mix on a superficial level, but they could never communicate. Recalling his youth in the Midwest, Nock believed that there had been a time in America when both peoples, although aware of their diverse cultures, had managed to maintain an amiable but distant relationship; but times had changed. Nock seemed to suggest that the change lay in Jewish refusal to be kept down. Implicit in his remarks was the notion that in an earlier time, before mass democracy, the Jewish problem had been kept under control by the custodians of Anglo-Saxon culture. But with the revolt of the masses Jews had become far more aggressive, and Nock would not be surprised to see in America in his own lifetime the "Nuremburg Laws reenacted and enforced with vigor."[36]

Implying that prejudice was to be found in America principally among ignorant mass men, Nock offered no solutions. He merely described the situation, his function being to chart "quicksands and rock formations so that the piers of some future structure might be secure." It was an incredible performance. His disclaimer that he was merely serving as a cartographer was hardly convincing, since he admittedly knew of the simmering antagonism in America toward Jews. When some readers were astonished at his pernicious article and angered by his failure even to mention the menace of Nazi racism, he disdained to reply; in the article he had maintained that Jews would be peculiarly unable to understand his meaning.[37]

The significance of the article lies in the degree to which it put the seal on Nock's total alienation and the extent to which his elitism distorted his judgment and taste. Pretending that he wished to launch a meaningful dialogue whereby intelligent Americans might probe the bigotry that infested not merely the lower orders but all society, Nock, by his patronizing tone and open anti-Semitism, linked himself inescapably to disreputable elements in American society and cast suspicion on his conception of the superior Remnant.

With the *Atlantic* articles Nock had crossed into the world of slander and innuendo that clouded his last years. He constructed a theory that contradicted much of his early work by explaining the rise of statism as a product of immigration; immigrants who had come to America in great numbers from all parts of Europe after the Civil War had been bred to the idea that the state was master, and that unquestioning obedience was their first duty. These immigrants had been a "powerful adulterant" in the American population.[38]

This point in Nock's career is like the bitter and frustrating later years of Henry Adams, with whom Nock has been compared. Indeed, Nock can be seen as a twentieth-century Henry Adams. Nock's published writings, private journals, and correspondence all reflect the kind of cataclysmic vision that obsessed Adams. Like Nock, Adams had progressed from defense of democracy's potential to criticism of its failings, among them its pervasive materialism, and had gone on to venomous attacks on the Jew as a pivotal figure in the destruction of the American dream. *Jewish* had been for Adams what *Finkman* became for Nock, a synonym for avarice and materialism. When Nock lamented the presence of Jews and other undesirables in what he seemed to consider his private study, the New York Public Library, he echoed the fierce resentment of the elderly Adams against the presence of Jews in places that he loved, and on boats and trains.[39]

Anti-Semitism for Nock, as for Adams, did not remain a symbolic protest against the tawdry aspects of rambunctious capitalism. Nock came to see the Jew as a personal oppressor against whom he could vent his feelings of superfluousness and rejection. Adams was angered by the easy adaptation of the Jewish immigrant to the American world. "Not a Polish Jew," he wrote, "fresh from Warsaw or Cracow —not a furtive Yacoob or Ysaac still reeking of the Ghetto, snarling a weird Yiddish . . . but had a keener instinct, an intenser energy, and a freer hand than he—American of Americans." Nock's feelings were similar. For him, too, the Jews were successfully challenging the traditional occupations and authority of the old Western European stock for which he spoke. He was affronted by the "new-style editor" who seemed to "stand more in the cutthroat-competitive attitude of Marks Pasinsky, Moe Griesman and Hymie Salzman . . . in the heyday of the cloak-and-suit trade, forty years ago." He resented new "immigrant" reviewers who were incapable of recognizing "erudition and style." It was insulting for a man named Finkelbein or Finkelstein to presume to question Nock's judgment when it was obvious that the man had only a short acquaintance with America. These new types were for Nock what they had become for Adams, the embodiment of all the alien and destructive forces in a world that had no place for them.[40]

Both Adams and Nock had believed, as Adams put it, that democracy could "transmute its social power into the higher forms of thought" and encourage and reward distinction. But their own intellectual journeys had belied that faith, which had gradually weakened, un-

til disillusion convinced both that all of "the old formulae had failed."
As a young man Adams had often described himself as a radical demo-
crat, but later he saw himself as a "Conservative Christian Anarchist."
If Adams used the phrase to describe himself as representing the small
Anglo-Saxon elite before the invading barbarians of industrial Amer-
ica, Nock might also be called a conservative Christian anarchist.[41]

Henry Adams's last forebodings of futility and rejection preceded
those of Nock. Nock sympathized with and greatly admired Adams,
"probably the ablest member" of the family. He wrote that Adams,
"the educated man," had been confronted by a society that seemed to
him "ignorant that there is a thing called ignorance." The limitations of the American character had finally driven the "student of
civilized man to despair," just as it had Nock. Nock applauded Adams's
assertions that he had only one idea left, "to get out of the world" as
fast as he could, and that he no longer cared if the world had gone to
the devil; it would "serve it right." Nock echoed these sentiments: "I
say let's go fast and straight and get it over with." Their ideals and
visions having degenerated into prejudices, both men, abandoning their
former beliefs, became prophets of decadence and doom, dedicated to
recording the fall of civilization.[42]

Nock spent the late thirties as a regular columnist for the *American
Mercury*, which had fallen on evil times even before Mencken's resignation in 1933. Paul Palmer, a wealthy newspaperman, had turned it
into an outspoken organ of conservative thought that specialized in
attacking Roosevelt. A great admirer of Nock's work, Palmer had
persuaded Nock to write a regular column on current affairs, "The
State of the Union." As close collaborators they turned the *Mercury*
into a monthly expression of Cram's ideas as applied by Nock to the
current scene. The *Mercury* printed, in its entirety, Cram's article,
"Why We Do Not Behave like Human Beings," along with an introduction by the editors describing it as "one of the most important
contributions ever made to an American magazine."[43]

Besides Nock's monthly assault on the swineries of New Deal domestic legislation, Nock and Palmer attacked liberal support of
Roosevelt's foreign policy. Month after month Nock ridiculed criticism of Hitler; Americans, he argued, were encouraged to see oppres-
sors in every corner of the earth by listening to sleazy politicians in

Washington who egged them on "by saying that 'we must lead the world.' " After a brief visit to Europe in the winter of 1937/38, Nock was sure that there would be no war. Disgruntled and confused, he published his last piece for the *Mercury* in September 1939, just before war broke out in Europe. England would not be attacked, he wrote, if she minded her own business. Since that was unlikely, he hoped Americans would "take a seat in the grandstand." By this time both Nock and Palmer began to feel that their work was futile. "You, and I, Mr. Nock," Palmer lamented, "seem to be about the only individualists left in the world. Everyone else you might say is a fascist." Nock left the *Mercury* in 1939 when Palmer, his fellow champion of the Remnant, repaired to the *Reader's Digest*, which, Palmer wrote, was trying in the face of overwhelming odds to bring sanity to a country moving toward war. There Palmer would continue to bring "the word" to the "morons" peopling America.[44]

Still seeking a Remnant, Nock turned to the subscribers to *Scribner's Commentator*, an abusive periodical that mixed Nazi apologia with anti-Semitic propaganda. In the month before Pearl Harbor, Nock declared that "the one big thundering reason" for Nazi hatred of the United States is "that we have blackguarded them incessantly and given all the aid and comfort to their enemies that we possibly could."[45]

Scribner's Commentator, which had attracted such notorious Nazi propagandists as Joseph E. McWilliams, Seward Collins, Fred Kister, and Gerald L. K. Smith, stopped publication, after the bombing of Pearl Harbor, with a call for patriotism and support of the government. Nock, convinced more than ever by the nation's entrance into the war that the state was a vehicle for bloodshed and tyranny, did not give up. Since most editors would no longer accept his work, he turned to book reviewing for the *Economic Council Review of Books*, circulated by the National Economic Council, an organization long associated with extreme right-wing causes. Founded by Merwin Kimball Hart, a wealthy Harvard graduate who had made a name for himself as a defender of Franco, the council offered a platform for the lunatic-fringe organizations opposing the war effort.[46]

Nock now found much of the Remnant, composed of people whose views had nothing in common with his anarchic views, enmeshed in the thicket of hysterical reaction. Though he scorned causes and crusaders, he had often come to the support of frustrated dissidents of dubious character. When questioned by his well-meaning friend and patron, Mrs. Evans, about some of the activities of the National Economic Council, Nock did not respond with his usual diffidence. Clearly irritated, he pointed out that he was not a member of the council. He merely wrote book reviews for it, in which he had a completely free hand; anyhow, it was a nonpartisan organization that stood for all the things he stood for. It was against collective statism, and its general views reflected the tradition of Jefferson, Franklin, Spencer, Emerson, and Thoreau. In his defense this self-professed anarchist who for years had characterized the Constitution as a vehicle of exploitation used what he had earlier called an imposter term, maintaining that the council was simply fighting for the restoration of constitutional government. The contradictions no longer mattered, in the heat of battle.[47]

The battle was no longer important to Nock, for the outbreak of war in Europe had ended his journalistic career. His book reviewing and correspondence had allowed him to let off steam after leaving the *Mercury*. He was not conscious of having abandoned his quest for Rabelaisian equanimity. His major work in this period—*Henry George*, published in 1939, and the *Memoirs*, in 1943—showed a remarkable ability to retreat into a contemplative world where he could shape ideas and abstractions to meet his personal needs and the dimensions of his unique vision.

His study of George is a beautifully written and at the same time perverse portrait of a tragic failure. George, Nock wrote, was "one of the first half-dozen of the world's creative geniuses in social philosophy." George's work, along with Herbert Spencer's, offered the "complete formulation of the philosophy of human freedom." Nothing substantial had ever been written to refute them, yet George, as well as Spencer, was a forgotten man.[48]

The impassioned Henry George who championed the common man and whose entire work was motivated by his desire to right the world's wrongs is not the hero of the book. On the contrary, he is the villain who brought about the failure of a potentially great and enduring Henry George. The latter George, wholly created by Nock, is a philosophical machine, able to see things as they really are. But the marvelously observant George was betrayed by George the activist who insisted that knowledge could be applied to the problems of the world. This notion, fortified by an incurable faith in man's desire and capacity to improve himself and society, led George the philosophical genius to dissipate his energy in a futile attempt to educate uneducable mass man. Thus George became involved in politics, causes, and crusades when he should have worked in Isaiah's vineyard for an elite Remnant. George had not understood that "the world's great philosophers never contemplated a mass-acceptance of themselves or their doctrines, but only their acceptance by an élite." But for George's fatal disabilities of temperament, his humanitarianism, his belief in political action, and his crusading spirit, he might have become prophet to the Remnant in a perfect society without a state.[49]

If George was dead and forgotten, there was, since Rabelais, one man who had achieved equanimity—Nock's creation, the hero of *Memoirs of a Superfluous Man*. It was a remarkable book. Written during World War II, it was a testament to one man's monumental pride. In it Nock portrayed himself as a superfluous man, who had seen from an early age the incredible stupidity of most men and had never been tempted by their vain hopes and aspirations. Instead of righting the world's evils, he had cultivated his own garden.

From his "seat in the grandstand" Nock described himself as an unperturbed spectator casually amused by events but never seriously concerned. There is no mention of his role on the *American Magazine* except a suggestion that even at that time he had understood the futility of all reform. Ignoring his eloquent pacifism, his search for a moral equivalent for war, and his vote for Wilson in 1916, he recalled having attributed no more than a casual significance to the war, since "when one has known for forty years precisely how a society's course of rebarbarisation must turn out in the long-run, one does not waste one's attention on day-to-day incidents of its progress."[50]

Quite in keeping with his anarchical theories was Nock's refusal to be bound by chronology. Before the mid-point of the *Memoirs of a Superfluous Man* he detailed his conversion to the ideas of Cram, thus giving readers the impression that Cram's views had been part of his mental equipment at the start of his career as a writer. Perhaps this was not a deception, for his earlier stance as a champion of enlightenment seems to have rested on a profoundly elitist base. Whether that is the case or not, the *Memoirs* are written from Nock's post-Cram point of view, so that all the events of his life are seen as shaped by his anarchist-elitist vision.

Monumentally conceited and arrogant, the *Memoirs of a Superfluous Man* is a wonderfully provocative work. William Harlowe Briggs, Nock's editor at Harper's, had been delighted by the title and the proposed anarchical format, which relieved Nock of all "responsibility —either moral or intellectual." Nock's splendid audacity, outrageous prejudice, and flamboyant iconoclasm stood in direct contrast to the degrading realities of human life in the 1940s and to the flagging spirits of those who were appalled by man's inhumanity to man. Nock's pride, his certainty as to the nature of man, and the catastrophic future he foresaw were his cathartic release from the real world. Along with his apocalyptic tone there was throughout a defiant, buoyant gaiety, a testament of the ability of one man to confront destruction with abandon and an almost jocular repudiation of all who hoped to turn back the tide.

Writing of a dead friend, Nock described what he believed to be his own state of exalted detachment:

> He was beyond the reach of disappointment or injury. His immense wisdom and penetrating humour, untouched by any taint of cynicism . . . kept him in the spirit which appears throughout all Greek literature; the spirit which finds its noblest expression in the *Phaedo*, and its more special and restricted expression in the verse of the later elegiac poets. He . . . had Aeschylus and Sophocles always at hand to remind him that the order fixed by human destiny is not to be coerced or dissuaded, and he [could watch] the hopeful little meddlings and strivings of the human comedy with an eye of amused tolerance, even as they ran off into inevitable tragedy.[51]

Ideals contemplated in themselves, as Ernest Sutherland Bates once observed, do indeed have a formal beauty. Even a philosophy of negation takes on a positive aspect when articulated with such intensity. If not in life, at least in his *Memoirs* Nock achieved the nobility of a free spirit in that shadowy realm where words do duty for things.[52]

Epilogue

WHILE NOCK WAS "throwing in the rough stuff" during the last stages of his *Memoirs of a Superfluous Man*, he wrote Paul Palmer that the best he could do was "hang on long enough to get through with it" but that he was not much interested beyond that. He spent the remaining two years of his life—he died in August 1945—for the most part confined to his study and convinced that the apocalypse was at hand. He corresponded vigorously with a small group of friends who agreed with him that Western society was declining so fast that the best one could do was sit back and enjoy the debacle. His correspondents' letters, to him and others, reflect the same feeling of pending doom accompanied by resignation.[1]

These letters shed a vivid light on the defection of once liberal men of good will from the social revolution that began during the New Deal. Nock's old friend of muckraker days, Lincoln Colcord, was convinced that America was well on the road to serfdom, and his attitude was one "of watching the show." Oswald Garrison Villard, an old "fighting liberal," wrote that he felt utterly out of place in the world. Dorothy Thompson, no longer a fervent internationalist, waited for "total disintegration": the bomb, she wrote, "offers peace, the peace of final clean destruction." Charles Beard, now beyond the pale for his opposition to Roosevelt's foreign policy, wondered what use there was in writing history since nobody learned anything from it. He declared, in a tone reminiscent of Twain, that his "resignation from the human race" still held good.[2]

It must have given Nock some comfort to have company during his gloomy vigil, although he denied caring one way or the other and was looking forward to the end of his life. He was delighted with the favorable comments his book received and astonished by its three printings in its first year. But he realized that it was praised more for style than for ideas. His theories, he felt, had hardly been discussed or even examined, but that was to be expected.[3]

Interest in Nock's work began to revive only a decade after his death. By the mid-fifties his books were being quoted in mass media. The *Memoirs of a Superfluous Man*, frequently and favorably compared to Henry Adams's *Education*, had become far less superfluous than Nock had imagined. In 1964 the Henry Regnery Company republished the *Memoirs*, along with an able, sympathetic exposition of his ideas. A volume of his letters was brought out in 1962 by the Caxton Printers, publishers of such champions of laissez-faire individualism as Ayn Rand, Rose Wilder Lane, Herbert Spencer, and William Graham Sumner. Nock's *Jefferson* reappeared in a paperback edition in 1960 and was acclaimed by a distinguished scholar as "the most captivating single volume in the Jefferson literature," the work of "a brilliant editor and a connoisseur of taste and intellect." In the 1950s when the *National Review* was struggling to attain its present influential circulation, it offered a collection of Nock's essays, *Snoring as a Fine Art*, as a lure to new subscribers, and as late as the winter of 1968 the *National Review*'s editor, William Buckley, Jr., lectured in that bastion of liberalism, the New School for Social Research, on Nock's theory of education.[4]

At first the interest in Nock seemed to be confined to a small body of eccentric conservative libertarians who championed his cause in obscure subterranean journals. He was revived as a prophet of the Remnant. Reflective and philosophical libertarians formed a Nockian Society, choosing as their patrons François Rabelais, Artemus Ward, and H. L. Mencken. It was no coincidence that the society's headquarters were in the offices of Leonard Read's Foundation for Economic Education, for the foundation had been organized to carry on the fight against "State interventionism—popularly called socialism, communism, Fabianism, nazism, the welfare state, the planned economy," or whatever was seen to threaten individual liberty. The foundation reproduced Nock's essay, "Isaiah's Job," to bolster sufferers from the "libertarian blues" lest they succumb to the temptation to "set the world straight."[5]

It would be a mistake, however, to conclude that Nock's ideas have become the exclusive property of a small cult of struggling libertarians and economic conservatives. Much of what he had to say is now recognized as being relevant to the American political, social, and cultural dialogue from "right" to "left," for, as Professor Murray Rothbard has put it, "The present-day categories of 'left' and 'right' have become misleading and obsolete," because partisans on either side recognize in the state the greatest menace to freedom.[6]

It has already been suggested that the increasing opposition to the state no longer comes only from its traditional critics, economic and political conservatives. Nock's dissent, in strikingly similar language, has become the dissent of spokesmen from all quarters of the contemporary political scene. James Reston of the *New York Times* has expressed his fear of the "overwhelming power of the executive." Daniel Moynihan, a sociologist, has warned fellow members of the liberal Americans for Democratic Action that they must lay aside the notion that the nation's problems can be solved by administrative agencies in Washington. A radical historian at Wisconsin, William Appleman Williams, has warned fellow radicals that they have reached a dead end by accepting a "centralized and consolidated" corporate state and that the "core radical . . . values of community, equality, democracy, and humaneness simply cannot . . . be realized . . . through more centralization and consolidation." In much of the debate over this peculiar merger of traditional foes, Nock's position is advanced. In a recent plea that the Old Right—that is, libertarian individualists like Nock—and the New Left recognize their common ground, Carl Oglesby, former president of Students for a Democratic Society, warned that to miss the meeting would mean that "the superstate will glide onward in its steel and vinyl splendor, tagging and numbering us with its scientific tests, conscripting us with computers, swaggering through exotic graveyards which it filled and where it dares to lay wreaths, smug in the ruins of its old-fashioned, man-centered promises to itself."[7]

It is ironic that Nock's place in the contemporary dialogue is in this kind of social criticism. He was not a historian, sociologist, or political pundit. He was primarily a cultural critic and therefore closer to the anarchically inclined younger radicals than to the older generation of liberals, disillusioned by the impotence and sterility of traditional politics. It may be difficult to imagine a bond between Nock and the bearded romantics of the 1960s. But Nock had called for such an anarchic band in 1930; he was scornful of the "elderly young" who acquiesced in the middle-class values of their parents and hoped to find "the youth of the land all ablaze with fire and brimstone, signing manifestos, starting newspapers, burning the whole Administration in effigy"—a prophetic description of the contemporary youthful revolt against authority. One can almost imagine Nock as an ancient guru, somewhat like Herbert Marcuse, instructing youth in the ways of cultural revolution. Certainly he would have been delighted by their anti-politics and unstructured, disorganized protest.[8]

It is almost as if Nock's Remnant had returned, for the anarchistic revolt by contemporary radicals against authority, the state, and the mechanistic manipulation of technological society is not without its own elitism. Seventy-year-old Marcuse, the unofficial philosopher of the New Left, has written a complicated philosophical critique of society that conforms in many of its particulars to the grim warnings of Nock. Marcuse's *One-Dimensional Man* is a technical analysis of Nock's mass man who has been systematically "moronized" by the state. Marcuse argues that the productive apparatus of technological society has "obliterated the opposition between the private and public existence, between individual and social needs." The resulting "one-dimensional man" can only recognize himself in his possessions. He finds his "soul in his automobile, hi-fi set, split level home, kitchen equipment." But most menacing of all, and completely compatible with Nock's analysis, is Marcuse's insistence that contemporary mass man is no longer conscious of the meaning of human freedom and individual self-determination. The state insures a high measure of material satisfaction, which mass man has come to identify with the good life; Nock described this as the worst aspect of modern civilization.[9]

More to the point is the self-flattering assurance of Marcuse and his acolytes that they have been granted a perception of reality and a "transcendent knowledge of good and evil, truth and falsity, human freedom and the good society" that has been withheld from most of their fellow citizens. Like the early Nock of the *Freeman*, the young, anarchic rebels speak out in compassion to the dispossessed. In traditional radical rhetoric they, too, denounce manipulative mass media, which Nock bitterly described as an "enormous army of commercial enterprisers" using every device of ingenuity to insure a docile, unthinking citizenry no longer aware of the values of freedom. They, like Nock, are dismayed by the growth of bureaucracies that are un-responsive to human needs and opposed to any participation by an individual in the decisions that shape his existence. To contemporary young radicals, only minority groups and the poor are outside of the brutal mass society described vividly by Nock. But as Michael Har-rington, a sympathetic critic, has pointed out, "if everybody but the poor and outcast are 'them,' then 'we' must inevitably lose, for by definition 'we' are not strong enough to transform a fraud and scandal supported by 60 or 70 percent of the society."[10]

What will happen if the prophetic minority cannot persuade the majority that the good society must be built according to their uncor-rupted vision? What is to prevent the new anarchists from acting out the same kind of tragic morality that led men like Albert Jay Nock into a world of misanthropic elitism, where words do duty for things?

Notes
Bibliography
Index

Notes

[*Full bibliographic information is given only for titles not listed in the Bibliography.*]

Preface

1. Albert Jay Nock, "Miscellany," *Freeman* 8 (20 Feb. 1924):560. See Stanley M. Elkins, *Slavery: A Problem in American Institutional and Intellectual Life* (New York, 1963); George M. Fredrickson, *The Inner Civil War: Northern Intellectuals and the Crisis of the Union* (New York, 1965).

2. Frederickson, *The Inner Civil War*, p. 10. And pp. 11–12. Nietzsche quoted in Francis Neilson, *How Diplomats Make War* (1961), p. 92.

3. Murray Rothbard, "Left and Right: The Prospects for Liberty," *Left and Right: A Journal of Libertarian Thought* 1 (spring 1965):16–17; Ronald Hamowy, "Left and Right Meet," *New Republic* 154 (12 Mar. 1966):15; Eric Goldman, "Aristocratic Dogma," *New York Times Book Review*, 29 Nov. 1964, p. 10; Hugh MacLennan, "Speaking of Books," *New York Times Book Review*, 30 Sept. 1962, p. 2; John Reed, *The Day in Bohemia, or Life among the Artists*, privately printed (Riverside, Conn., 1913), copy of excerpts given to me by Robert M. Crunden; Clinton Rossiter, *Conservatism in America* (1962), p. 169; Louis Filler, ed., *The Anxious Years* (New York, 1963), p. 49. Rossiter also mentions Nock on p. 159.

1. The Anarchist Tradition

1. Benj. R. Tucker, *Instead of a Book*, p. 14.
2. George Woodcock, *Anarchism*, pp. 33, 49–50.
3. Emma Goldman, *Living My Life* (New York, 1931), p. 556.
4. Tucker, *Instead of a Book*, p. 404.
5. Ibid., p. 370.
6. Ibid., p. 31.
7. Quoted in Eunice Minette Schuster, *Native American Anarchism*, p. 56.
8. Frederick Jackson Turner, "The Significance of the Frontier in American History," *The Frontier in American History* (New York, 1921), p. 38; Henry F. May, *The End of American Innocence* (Quadrangle Books, Chi-

cago, 1964), p. 306; Emma Goldman, "Minorities versus Majorities," *Anarchism and Other Essays* (New York, 1911), p. 84.

9. Eastman quoted in Daniel Aaron, *Writers on the Left: Episodes in American Literary Communism* (New York, 1961), pp. 83, 61; Emma Goldman, *Living My Life*, p. 194.

10. Richard Drinnon, *Rebel in Paradise*, p. 158. And Judith Shklar, *After Utopia: The Decline of Political Faith* (Princeton, 1957), p. 101.

11. William Harlowe Briggs to Nock, 7 Nov. 1941, Miscellaneous Correspondence, Palmer Papers; Nock to Paul Palmer, 7 Aug. 1942, Palmer Papers.

12. Nock, "The Purpose of Biography," *Snoring as a Fine Art*, p. 121; Van Wyck Brooks, *Days of the Phoenix*, p. 54.

13. Interview with Ruth Robinson, 18 Apr. 1964; A. A. Boyden to Nock, Nov. 1915, Palmer Papers. And "Autobiographical Sketch of Albert Jay Nock," written for Paul Palmer, Crunden Papers.

14. Nock, *Journal of These Days*, 14 Dec. 1933, p. 292; and to Bernard Iddings Bell, n.d., Crunden Papers.

15. Tucker, *Instead of a Book*, p. 15; Nock, *Memoirs of a Superfluous Man* (1964), p. 307.

16. Nock, *Journal of These Days*, 30 Dec. 1932, p. 104. And Robert M. Crunden, *The Mind and Art of Albert Jay Nock*, chap. 1, passim; Nock, "Autobiographical Sketch."

17. Nock, *Memoirs*, pp. 32, 28; *New York Times*, 30 June 1866, quoted in Harold Coffin Syrett, *The City of Brooklyn, 1865–1898* (New York, 1944), p. 18.

18. Nock, *Memoirs*, pp. 57, 60.

19. Ibid., pp. 46–47. And p. 14.

20. Ibid., p. 50. And pp. 49–51.

21. Ibid., pp. 66, 79; Nock, "The Vanished University," *Freeman* 3 (29 June 1921):364. And Nock, *Memoirs*, pp. 65, 67–71, 75–78, 80–85, and "On American Education," *Free Speech and Plain Language*, p. 189.

22. Paul Goodman, *Compulsory Mis-education and The Community of Scholars* (Vintage Books, New York, 1964), p. 162; descriptions of college and faculty, Addison's judgment, and criticism by the Society for the Promotion of Religion and Learning are quoted in a letter of Richard Gummere, Jr., to Crunden, 27 July 1961, Crunden Papers.

23. Nock, *Memoirs*, pp. 82–83; Peter P. Witonski, "Albert Jay Nock and the St. Stephen's Tradition," *Bard College* (winter 1966); Witonski article in clippings file, Crunden Papers.

24. Nock, *Memoirs*, p. 52. And Nock, "Anarchist's Progress," *On Doing the Right Thing*, pp. 123–28.

25. Nock, *Memoirs*, p. 30.

26. *The Catalogue of the Berkeley Divinity School, 1895–96*, lists Nock as a member of the "Middle Class of 1896"; in the 1909 catalogue he is listed as a nongraduate who did not complete the course but was afterwards ordained; Francis J. Nock to Professor Fine (?), 27 Feb. 1958, Robinson Papers; Francis Nock to Crunden, 11 Apr. 1962, Crunden Papers, mentions Nock's alleged baseball playing. This story has been repeated by a number of his friends and by students of Nock's life and work, but I have never discovered any substantial evidence of its accuracy.

27. Miss Robinson's observation on the great influence of Nock's mother appears in "Memo for Biographical First Chapter," Crunden Papers.

28. A brief clerical biography may be found in *Stowes Clerical Directory of the American Church, 1920–21* (Minneapolis, Minn.), p. 198; see also the brief history of Nock's ministry at St. James, in the Crunden Papers.

29. For the anecdote see Francis Jay Nock to Robinson, 23 Aug. 1945, Robinson Papers.

30. Conversation with the Rev. Robert H. Moore, Meadville, Pa., 14 Nov. 1970. Mr. Moore is an Episcopal clergyman and an enthusiastic member of the Nockian Society. He has taken an interest in Nock's clerical past and managed to dig up some information about Nock's tenure at Titusville.

31. History of Nock's ministry at St. James, Crunden Papers. For brief notes on Nock's parish duties see "Parochial Report," *Journal of the Thirty-sixth Annual Convention of the Protestant Episcopal Church in the Diocese of Pittsburgh, 1901*, p. 41. Diocesan journals may be found at the General Theological Seminary in New York City.

32. Roger A. Walke, Jr., rector, Christ Episcopal Church, Blacksburg, Va., to Crunden, 16 Apr. 1962, Crunden Papers. This letter gives dates of Nock's tenure but no information about his ministry. See also "Parochial Report," *Journal of the Twelfth Annual Convention of the Protestant Episcopal Church in the Diocese of Western Virginia, 1905*, p. 183 (only the dates of his service in Blacksburg and perfunctory parish reports appear in the convention journals). Otto Koch, treasurer of St. Joseph's Church, has confirmed for me the dates of Nock's ministry in Detroit, from 3 Sept. 1907 until his resignation on 9 July 1909. For reference to Nock's nonparish status see J. Sandor Cziraky, *The Evolution of the Social Philosophy of Albert Jay Nock*, p. 15. See also *Journal of the Proceedings of the Seventy-fifth Annual Convention of the Protestant Episcopal Church in the Diocese of Michigan,*

1910, pp. 15, 29, 202. In many of these church records Nock is credited with a Ph.D. degree, although there is no record of his having received one. He did receive an honorary doctorate much later from St. Stephen's.

33. Nock, "The Value to the Clergyman of Training in the Classics," *School Review* 16 (June 1908): 385, 384, 389.

34. Nock, *Memoirs*, p. 292; for evidence of his Detroit friendship see Robinson, "Autobiographical Notes," p. 8; Nock to Robinson, 10 June 1913, 14 Dec. 1913, Robinson Papers. Miss Robinson deposited at Yale University two books of poetry that were a gift to Nock while in Detroit from his friend. Nock's cryptic letter describing what would have happened if he had taken up the ministry may be found in Nock to Robinson, 31 Dec. 1912, Robinson Papers.

35. Nock, *Memoirs*, p. 295. And Robinson, "Autobiographical Notes," p. 3, Robinson Papers; author's interview with Miss Robinson, 18 Apr. 1964.

36. Nock, *Memoirs*, pp. 208, 209, 211. A former associate of Nock's who wishes to remain anonymous believes that Nock did remarry privately.

37. Nock to Robinson, 28 June 1913, Robinson Papers.

38. Robinson, "Autobiographical Notes," p. 8, Robinson Papers; and "Typescript of Autobiographical Sketch," written for Paul Palmer, Crunden Papers. Miss Robinson was always fascinated by Nock's secretive ways and at one point described them as a "compulsive deviousness" (for want of a better description, she said), in a collection of "odd notes," Robinson Papers.

39. Woodcock, *Anarchism*, p. 34.

2. The Genteel Muckraker

1. To Ruth Robinson, 4 Apr. 1912, in Francis J. Nock, ed., *Selected Letters of Albert Jay Nock*, p. 23.

2. To Robinson, 16 Jan. 1911, *Selected Letters*, p. 16.

3. To Brand Whitlock, 29 Aug. 1912, *Selected Letters*, p. 27.

4. Randolph Bourne to Carl Zigrosser, 3 Nov. 1913, quoted in Christopher Lasch, *The New Radicalism in America*, p. 81; Nock to Robinson, 1 Jan. 1914, *Selected Letters*, p. 51.

5. Nock, Introduction to Brand Whitlock, *Forty Years of It*, p. xii; carbon of original manuscript, dated 20 Nov. 1913, Palmer Papers; Nock, "Brand Whitlock," *American Magazine* 69 (Mar. 1910): 599.

6. Lionel Trilling, *Matthew Arnold* (1939), p. 254; Matthew Arnold, "Numbers; or, The Majority and the Remnant," *Discourses in America*

(London, 1885), p. 31; Nock, Introduction to Whitlock, *Forty Years*, p. x; to Whitlock, 29 Aug. 1912, *Selected Letters*, pp. 26–27.

7. To Whitlock, 29 Aug. 1912, *Selected Letters*, p. 27. See also William G. McLoughlin, "Pietism and the American Character," *American Quarterly* 17 (summer 1965): 165 ff., for an analysis of the pietistic radical tradition in America.

8. Nock, Introduction to Whitlock, *Forty Years*, p. xii.

9. Ibid., p. 239; Bourne quoted in Lasch, *The New Radicalism*, p. 254; Nock, "Is It True?" *American Magazine* 75 (Jan. 1913): 54; to Robinson, 31 Dec. 1912, 28 June 1913, *Selected Letters*, pp. 28, 36.

10. To Robinson, 29 Jan. 1913, 18 June 1913, *Selected Letters*, pp. 30, 33, 34.

11. Ray Stannard Baker, *American Chronicle*, pp. 226, 227.

12. Nock, "Henry George: Unorthodox American," *Snoring as a Fine Art*, p. 86; and "A Tax on Ignorance and Honesty," *American Magazine* 71 (Dec. 1910): 148, 150.

13. Nock, "Taxes Two Sides of the Line," *American Magazine* 72 (May 1911): 78–79. And "Why Nature's Way is Best," *American Magazine* 72 (July, 1911): 338.

14. Nock, *Henry George: An Essay*, pp. 150, 174; see Eunice Minette Schuster, *Native American Anarchism*, p. 136, for connection between anarchists and single-taxers.

15. Nock, "What We All Stand For," *American Magazine* 75 (Feb. 1913): 53–57.

16. Ibid., p. 54.

17. Jacques Barzun, ed., *The Selected Writings of John Jay Chapman* (New York, 1957), p. v; M. A. DeWolfe Howe, *John Jay Chapman and His Letters* (Boston, 1937), pp. 215–16.

18. Richard Hofstadter, *Anti-Intellectualism in American Life* (1966), p. 359; John Dewey, *Democracy and Education* (New York, 1961 [New York, 1916]), p. 79; for discussion of Dewey's conception of education as a means to utopianism or social control, see Lasch, *The New Radicalism*, pp. 158 ff.

19. Hofstadter, *Anti-Intellectualism*, p. 362; Nock, *Memoirs* (1964), p. 47; Lawrence A. Cremin, *The Transformation of the School: Progressivism in American Education, 1876–1957* (New York, 1961), p. ix.

20. Nock, "An Adventure in Education," *American Magazine* 77 (Apr. 1914): 26; Randolph S. Bourne, "Schools in Gary," *New Republic* 2 (27 Mar. 1915): 199; Nock, loc. cit., p. 27. And Bourne, loc. cit., p. 198. The discussion that follows is based on Nock's article, pp. 25–28.

21. Lasch, *The New Radicalism*, pp. 13–14.

22. Lippmann, *Drift and Mastery: An Attempt to Diagnose the Current Unrest* (Englewood Cliffs, N.J., 1961 [New York, 1914]), p. 98.

23. Bourne to Dorothy Teall, 4 June 1915, in *The World of Randolph Bourne*, p. 306; Lippmann, *Drift and Mastery*, p. 43.

24. Lippmann, *Drift and Mastery*, p. 43; Louis D. Brandeis, *Business—A Profession* (Boston, 1914), p. 2; see also pp. 12, 57 ff.; Lippmann, *Drift and Mastery*, p. 44.

25. To Robinson, 6 Jan. 1914, *Selected Letters*, p. 53.

26. Nock, "Motherhood and the State," *Atlantic Monthly* 114 (Aug. 1914):157–63; see also Lasch, *The New Radicalism*, pp. 49–56, for an interesting analysis of these ideas.

27. To Robinson, 4 Sept. 1914, *Selected Letters*, p. 68.

28. To Robinson, 23 Apr. 1914, 2 and 3 Aug. 1914, *Selected Letters*, pp. 60, 63, 64.

29. To Robinson, 17 Sept. 1914, *Selected Letters*, p. 70. And p. 69, and 4 Sept. 1914, p. 68; Lincoln Steffens, *The Autobiography of Lincoln Steffens* (New York, 1931), pp. 575–76; Baker, *American Chronicle*, p. 302; Nock, "Edison in War Time," *American Magazine* 78 (Nov. 1914):33–38.

30. To Robinson, 4 Sept. 1914, 21 June 1911, 29 Jan. 1913, 20 Nov. 1913, *Selected Letters*, pp. 67, 18, 31, 39. And to Robinson, 31 Dec. 1912, 2 Aug. 1914, pp. 28–29, 63; to Whitlock, 29 Aug. 1912, p. 26. See also Robert M. Crunden, *A Hero in Spite of Himself: Brand Whitlock in Art, Politics, and War* (New York, 1969), p. 179.

3. The Journalist as Philosophicker

1. To Ruth Robinson, 2 and 3 Aug. 1914, *Selected Letters*, pp. 63, 64.

2. Nock, "World Scouts," *American Magazine* 73 (Jan. 1912):275–84.

3. Nock to Robinson, 9 Sept. 1914, *Selected Letters*, p. 69; Nock, "In the Interpreter's House: How the War Has Opened a Business Opportunity to America," *American Magazine* 78 (Nov. 1914):64.

4. William James, "The Moral Equivalent of War," in *Memories and Studies* (London, 1911, pp. 286–92; Randolph Bourne, "A Moral Equivalent for Universal Military Service," *New Republic* 7 (1 July 1916):217–19; Nock, "In the Interpreter's House: Why Not Keep a Standing Army—Not to Fight Men, But to Fight Flies, Rats, and Other Real Enemies?" *American Magazine* 78 (Dec. 1914):65–66, 70–71.

5. Nock, "Interpreter's House," *American Magazine* 78 (Dec. 1914):66.

6. Randolph Bourne, "The State," in *The World of Randolph Bourne*, p. 250; "A Moral Equivalent," p. 218.

7. Nock, "In the Interpreter's House: To His Imperial Majesty Nicholas II, Emperor and Autocrat of All the Russias," *American Magazine* 79 (Feb. 1915):62. Bernhardi's *Germany and the Next War* was translated into English in 1914.

8. Nock, "Interpreter's House: To . . . Nicholas II," *American Magazine* 79 (Mar. 1915):54; Nock to Robinson, 17 Sept. 1914, *Selected Letters*, p. 70.

9. Nock, "Interpreter's House," *American Magazine* 79 (Mar. 1915):54, 55, 82, 83.

10. Nock, "Peace the Aristocrat," *Atlantic Monthly* 115 (May 1915):593–99.

11. Nock to Robinson, 11 June 1915, *Selected Letters*, p. 79.

12. Charles Forcey, *The Crossroads of Liberalism*, p. 85.

13. Nock to Robinson, 23 Apr. 1914, *Selected Letters*, p. 60; Robert M. Crunden, *The Mind and Art of Albert Jay Nock*, p. 51. I believe that Crunden prematurely dates Nock's disillusionment concerning man's potential perfection with his article, "Peace the Aristocrat." On the contrary, it is a strong reaffirmation of man's ability to better his world.

14. Francis Neilson, "The Story of *The Freeman*," pp. 6–7; Crunden, *Mind and Art of Nock*, p. 12; Allan Nevins, ed., *The Journal of Brand Whitlock* (New York, 1936), p. 93; Nock to Robinson, 11 June 1915, *Selected Letters*, p. 79.

15. Neilson, *How Diplomats Make War* (New York, 1915), pp. 6, 10, 373; Nock, Introduction to *How Diplomats Make War* (1915), pp. vi–vii. See also Nock, *The Myth of a Guilty Nation*.

16. Nock, "Prohibition in Kansas," *North American Review* 204 (Aug. 1916):261; "Prohibition and Civilization," *North American Review* 204 (Sept. 1916):407, 411.

17. 20 Sept. 1916, 15 Nov. 1915, *Selected Letters*, pp. 85, 81.

18. Editor's note, *Atlantic Monthly* 120 (July 1917):140; Nock to Ellery Sedgwick, 14 July 1917, *Selected Letters*, pp. 89–90.

19. To Robinson, 29 Sept. 1917, *Selected Letters*, pp. 93–94.

20. Frederic C. Howe, *The Confessions of a Reformer* (New York, 1925), pp. 280–82. For a brilliant critique of liberal and radical complicity in the dubious aspects of the warfare state, see Randolph Bourne, "Twilight of Idols," *Seven Arts* 2 (Oct. 1917):688–702. Bourne's antiwar essays are collected in *War and the Intellectuals*.

21. To Robinson, 15 Nov. 1915, *Selected Letters*, p. 81.

22. Ibid., 6 Jan. 1914, *Selected Letters*, p. 53; Nock, "What American Labor Does Not See," *Nation* 107 (24 Aug. 1918):195.

23. Nock, "The One Thing Needful," *Nation* 107 (14 Sept. 1918):283.

24. Oswald Garrison Villard, "Peace at Last," *Nation* 107 (16 Nov. 1918):572.

25. Nock and Villard, editorial paragraph, *Nation* 107 (10 Aug. 1918): 135; ibid., 107 (17 Aug. 1918):159 (authorship of unsigned editorials and articles in the *Nation* has been verified by checking them against the annotated set deposited by Villard in the New York Public Library); Nock, editorial paragraph, *Freeman* 4 (21 Sept. 1921):36 (all unsigned editorial paragraphs and articles attributed to Nock have been checked against the annotated set of the *Freeman* deposited in the Manuscript Division, Columbia University Library).

26. Nock, "The End and the Means," *Nation* 108 (22 Mar. 1919): 416–17.

27. Nock, "An Exhausted Virtue," *Nation* 108 (14 June 1919):929.

28. To Francis Neilson, 14 Nov. 1919, *Selected Letters*, p. 95.

29. Neilson, "The Story of *The Freeman*," pp. 19–21; Villard to Nock, 3 Nov. 1919, and Nock to Villard, 17 Nov. 1919, Villard Papers.

30. Quotation from the advertisement on the back cover of the first issue of the *Freeman* (17 Mar. 1920).

4. The Nobility of the Free Man

1. Nock, *Memoirs* (1964), p. 172. See also Van Wyck Brooks, *Days of the Phoenix*, pp. 56–57; Suzanne La Follette, Introduction to Nock, *Snoring as a Fine Art*, pp. vii–xi.

2. Editorial paragraph, *Nation* 110 (20 Mar. 1920):353; Nock, "In the Vein of Intimacy," *Freeman* 1 (31 Mar. 1920):52; Nock to Villard, 16 Mar. 1920, Villard Papers.

3. Nock, "Radical Activity," *Freeman* 1 (24 Mar. 1920):29; "In the Vein of Intimacy," p. 52.

4. Lewis Mumford, Letter to the Editor, *Freeman* 1 (24 Mar. 1920):34–35.

5. Francis Neilson, "The Story of *The Freeman*," passim; Nock, "To Whom It May Concern," *Freeman* 1 (16 June 1920):319–20; Nock, "Miscellany," *Freeman* 6 (11 Oct. 1922):111–12.

6. Quoted in James P. Lichtenberger, *Development of Social Theory* (New

York, 1923), p. 449. See also Leslie White, *The Science of Culture: A Study of Man and Civilization* (New York, 1949), p. 182, for the deterministic implications of Gumplowicz.

7. Franz Oppenheimer, *The State*.

8. Ibid., p. 25.

9. Ibid., pp. 285–86, 290. Oppenheimer later came to America and, along with Francis Neilson, was a founder of the *American Journal of Economics and Sociology*. It is supported by the Robert Schalkenbach Foundation, which to this day promotes the economic theories of Henry George.

10. Theodore Hertzka, *Freeland: A Social Anticipation* (London, 1891), p. xxi; Nock, "To Whom It May Concern," *Freeman* 1 (16 June 1920): 320.

11. Nock, "A Programme of Action," *Freeman* 3 (13 Apr. 1921): 100.

12. Ibid., p. 101.

13. Nock, editorial paragraph, *Freeman* 2 (29 Dec. 1920): 362.

14. Ibid. (27 Oct. 1920), p. 147; "So Shall Ye Reap," *Freeman* 5 (19 Apr. 1922): 125–26; "In Contempt of Court," *Freeman* 4 (21 Sept. 1921): 29.

15. Nock, "Culture and Freedom," *Freeman* 1 (8 Sept. 1920): 605; "The Logic of the Blue Laws," *Freeman* 2 (15 Dec. 1920): 316; "Miscellany," *Freeman* 6 (25 Oct. 1922): 159.

16. Nock, "A Job for a Despot," *Freeman* 2 (20 Oct. 1920): 127–28; Lillian Symes and Travers Clement, *Rebel America*, pp. 338–39.

17. Nock, "Editorial Reply," *Freeman* 1 (28 July 1920): 475.

18. Nock, "A Reviewer's Notebook," *Freeman* 5 (5 July 1922): 407. Nock replaced Van Wyck Brooks at the "Reviewer's Notebook" stand from 24 May 1922 to 10 Jan. 1923.

19. Nock to Ellery Sedgwick, 9 Aug. 1913, *Selected Letters*, p. 37. See Christopher Lasch, *The American Liberals and the Russian Revolution* (New York, 1962), p. 146.

20. Nock, "A Reviewer's Notebook," *Freeman* 5 (5 July 1922): 407; "A Problem of Definition," *Freeman* 4 (14 Sept. 1921): 4; "The Liberal Rabbinism," *Freeman* 5 (6 Sept. 1922): 604; "A Reviewer's Notebook," *Freeman* 6 (13 Sept. 1922): 23.

21. H. L. Mencken, "Letter to the Editor: A Definition of Democracy," *Freeman* 4 (28 Sept. 1921): 64; Nock, "The Critic and the Ordinary Man," *Freeman* 2 (10 Nov. 1920): 199–200; "Our Pastors and Masters," *Freeman* 3 (26 Jan. 1921): 461.

22. Nock, "The Critic and the Ordinary Man," p. 200; "A Cultural Forecast," *On Doing the Right Thing*, p. 93.

23. Nock, "The Critic and the Ordinary Man," p. 200.

24. Nock, "A Study in Literary Temper," *Freeman* 2 (26 Jan. 1921):464–67.

25. Ibid.

26. Lewis Mumford, "A Study in Social Distemper," *Freeman* 2 (9 Feb. 1921):519–20.

27. Ibid.

28. Nock, "A Study in Literary Criticism," *Freeman* 3 (16 Mar. 1921): 10–12.

29. Paul Rosenfeld, "Mr. Nock," in Rosenfeld, *Men Seen,* pp. 325–45.

30. Nock, "A Reviewer's Notebook," *Freeman* 6 (15 Nov. 1922):239. See also Nock, "Miscellany," *Freeman* 8 (24 Oct. 1923):151; Nock, "Miscellany," *Freeman* 7 (8 Aug. 1923):511; Susan Turner, *A History of the "Freeman,"* pp. 86, 136–37.

31. Nock, *Memoirs,* p. 169; Suzanne La Follette, Introduction to Nock, *Snoring as a Fine Art,* passim; Brooks, *Days of the Phoenix,* pp. 56–59.

32. Nock, "A Reviewer's Notebook," *Freeman* 5 (22 Aug. 1922):574–75; Harold Stearns, ed., *Civilization in the United States,* p. vii; George Soule, "Radicalism," in Stearns, *Civilization,* p. 273; John Dos Passos, "Whither the American Writer," *Modern Quarterly* 6 (summer 1932):11.

33. Nock, "A Misplaced Man," *Freeman* 7 (4 July 1923):388–89.

34. Nock, "The Vanished University," *Freeman* 3 (29 June 1921):364; Charles Beard, Letter to the editor, *Freeman* 3 (20 July 1921):450–51.

35. Nock, "Miscellany," Freeman 8 (14 Nov. 1923):223–24.

36. Ibid. (26 Dec. 1923), pp. 367–68.

37. Ibid. (19 Sept. 1923), p. 31; ibid. (26 Dec. 1923), pp. 367–68.

38. "Miscellany," *Freeman* 8 (19 Sept. 1923):32; Nock, "An Open Letter," *Freeman* 8 (27 Feb. 1924):582–83; "Miscellany," *Freeman* 8 (27 Feb. 1924):583–84.

39. "Morals of the Market Place," *Freeman* 8 (5 Mar. 1924): 607–8.

40. Ibid.

41. Nock, "Miscellany," *Freeman* 8 (6 Feb. 1924):512; "A Last Word to Our Readers," *Freeman* 8 (6 Feb. 1924):508; to Lincoln Colcord, 30 Sept. 1927, *Selected Letters,* p. 103.

5. The Freedom of Noble Men

1. Henry George to David A. Wells, 19 Sept. 1871, quoted in Joseph Dorfman, *The Economic Mind in American Civilization* (New York, 1949), 3: 143; Nock, "A Last Word to Our Readers," *Freeman* 8 (6 Feb. 1924):508.

See also Nock to Mrs. Edmund C. Evans, 29 Dec. 1924, *Letters* (to Mr. and Mrs. Evans and Ellen Winsor), p. 18. Mr. and Mrs. Evans and her sister, Miss Winsor, were wealthy Philadelphia subscribers to the *Freeman* and became patrons of Nock after the magazine ceased publication.

2. Nock to Mrs. Evans, 29 Dec. 1924, 6 Feb. 1926, *Letters*, pp. 18, 22.

3. Amos Pinchot, "Miscellany," *Freeman* 1 (17 Mar. 1920):15.

4. Nock to Mrs. Evans, 12 Jan. 1926, *Letters*, p. 20.

5. Nock, ed., *Selected Works of Artemus Ward*, pp. 13–16. This essay is reprinted in *On Doing the Right Thing*, pp. 1–24.

6. Nock, "Artemus Ward," *On Doing*, p. 24.

7. Nock, *Jefferson* (1960), p. 203; *Memoirs* (1964), pp. xi–xii; "The Purpose of Biography," *Snoring as a Fine Art*, passim.

8. Nock, *Jefferson*, pp. 3, 11.

9. Ibid., pp. 20, 56.

10. Ibid., pp. 27–28.

11. Ibid., pp. 123, 145, 159.

12. Ibid., pp. 55, 132.

13. Ibid., pp. 115–16, 67, 151. For an example of another side of Jefferson, totally ignored by Nock, see Leonard W. Levy, *Jefferson and Civil Liberties: The Darker Side* (Cambridge, Mass., 1963).

14. Nock, *Jefferson*, pp. 115–17. See also S[amuel] E[liot] Morison, "Thomas Jefferson Still Lives," *New Republic* 49 (15 Dec. 1926):115–16.

15. Nock, *Jefferson*, pp. 162–63.

16. Ibid., pp. 190–91.

17. Ibid., p. 194.

18. Nock, book review, *Saturday Review of Literature* 6 (11 Jan. 1930): 631; Stuart Sherman, "Thomas Jefferson: A Revaluation," *The Main Stream*, p. 31.

19. Mencken quoted in Frederick J. Hoffman, *The Twenties*, p. 307; Nock to Mrs. Evans, n.d., *Letters*, p. 26. See also Nock to Mrs. Evans, 24 July 1927, *Letters*, p. 36.

20. Nock to Mrs. Evans, n.d., *Letters*, p. 24; to Lincoln Colcord, 30 Sept. 1927, *Selected Letters*, p. 103; "On Making Low People Interesting" and "A Cultural Forecast," *On Doing*, pp. 65, 77.

21. Quoted in Hoffman, *The Twenties*, p. 308.

22. Ibid., p. 306; Nock, "Cultural Forecast," p. 93.

23. Nock, "Artemus Ward," "Cultural Forecast," and "Towards a New Quality-Product," pp. 9, 112, 80, 121.

24. Nock, "The Decline of Conversation," "New Quality-Product," and "Low People," pp. 114–15, 27, 67, 52.

25. "Low People," pp. 65, 66, 30, 66. See also Crunden, *A Hero in Spite of Himself: Brand Whitlock in Art, Politics, and War* (New York, 1969), p. 178; Montague Glass, *Potash and Perlmutter* (New York, 1909).

26. Nock, "Decline of Conversation," pp. 30, 32, 31, 39, 44, 33, 47. And pp. 34, 46.

27. Ibid., p. 45. For anti-Semitism in the twenties, see, e.g., John Higham, *Strangers in the Land: Patterns of American Nativism, 1860–1925* (New Brunswick, N.J., 1955), pp. 271–73; E. Digby Baltzell, *The Protestant Establishment*, pp. 222–25; William Manchester, *H. L. Mencken: Disturber of the Peace* (New York, 1962).

28. Nock, "Cultural Forecast," pp. 86, 87.

29. Nock, "New Quality-Product," p. 113.

30. Burton Rascoe, "A Bookman's Day Book," *New York Tribune*, 2 July 1922, pt. 5, p. 4; Nock, "A Reviewer's Notebook," *Freeman* 5 (19 July 1922):454–55.

31. The most pertinent to this discussion are: Irving Babbitt, *Literature and the American College* (Boston, 1908), *The New Laokoon* (Boston, 1910), *Rousseau and Romanticism* (Boston, 1919), *Democracy and Leadership* (Boston, 1924); Paul Elmer More, *Shelburne Essays*, 11 vols. (Boston, 1904–21). The *Shelburne Essays* contain the following relevant books: *The Drift of Romanticism* (Boston, 1913), *Aristocracy and Justice* (Boston, 1915), and *The Demon of the Absolute* (Princeton, 1928), which was the first volume in the *New Shelburne Essays*.

32. Norman Foerster, ed., *Humanism and America: Essays on the Outlook of Modern Civilization* (New York, 1930); C. Hartley Grattan, ed., *The Critique of Humanism: A Symposium* (New York, 1930). In addition to Babbitt and More, Humanists included in the Foerster collection were Harry Hayden Clarke, T. S. Eliot, Frank Jewett Mather, Jr., Louis Trenchard More (Paul Elmer's brother), and Gorham B. Munson. Stuart Sherman did not have an essay in the collection but was often included in the group. The most noted critics of Humanism in the Grattan anthology were R. P. Blackmur, Kenneth Burke, John Chamberlain, Malcolm Cowley, Allan Tate, Lewis Mumford, Edmund Wilson, and Yvor Winters. The Cowley statement is from his *Exile's Return* (New York, 1951), pp. 302–3.

33. Babbitt, *Democracy and Leadership*, pp. 26, 148–49; More, *The Demon of the Absolute*, p. 11. For particularly acute analyses see Hoffman, *The Twenties*, pp. 139–45; Alfred Kazin, *On Native Grounds: An Interpretation of Modern American Prose Literature* (New York, 1942), pp. 291–311; Allen Guttmann, *The Conservative Tradition in America*, pp. 135–41; David Spitz, *Patterns of Anti-Democratic Thought*, rev. ed. (New York,

1965); and Russell Kirk, *The Conservative Mind* (Chicago, 1953). I am indebted to all of these authors for helping me make my way through the tangled thickets of the Humanist argument.

34. Babbitt, "Humanism: An Essay in Definition," in *Humanism and America*, p. 33; More, *The Demon of the Absolute*, p. 23.

35. Norman Foerster, Preface to *Humanism and America*, p. vi; Cowley, "Humanizing America," in *Critique of Humanism*, p. 67.

36. Hoffman, *The Twenties*, p. 139; Lionel Trilling, *Matthew Arnold* (1949), pp. 342–43. The term "Christian kind of conduct" is Trilling's with respect to the morality of Arnold, but he makes a good case for the congeniality to the Humanists of this aspect of Arnold's thought. For T. S. Eliot's comments, see Guttmann, *Conservative Tradition*, pp. 137–38; Allen Tate, "The Fallacy of Humanism," in *Critique of Humanism*, pp. 160–66. For an early Nock statement about the compatibility of religion and Humanist classicism, see "The Value to the Clergyman of Training in the Classics," *School Review* 16 (June 1908):383–90.

37. Frank Jewett Mather, Jr., "The Plight of Our Arts," in *Humanism and America*, pp. 115–16; for Nock's discussion of a classical university, see discussion of his educational theories in Chapter 6. For a caustic appraisal of Humanist "utopianism" with respect to education, see Cowley, "Humanizing America," in *Critique of Humanism*, p. 70.

38. Babbitt, *Democracy and Leadership*, pp. 261, 265, 278; More, *Aristocracy and Justice*, p. 30; Babbitt, *Democracy and Leadership*, p. 8.

39. Trilling, *Matthew Arnold*, pp. 342–43, discusses Joubert's notion of negative morality and its appeal to Arnold and subsequently to the Humanists; Nock, *Memoirs* (1964), p. 303.

40. More, *Aristocracy and Justice*, p. 212; Nock, *Journal of These Days*, 24 Mar. 1933, p. 147; Mencken quoted in Hoffman, *The Twenties*, p. 143. For Babbitt's censure of Goethe, see "Humanism: An Essay at Definition," in *Humanism and America*, p. 48; for a modernist response, see Edmund Wilson, "Notes on Babbitt and More," and Cowley, "Humanizing America," in *Critique of Humanism*, pp. 48–49, 76.

41. Ralph Barton Perry, *Puritanism and Democracy* (New York, 1944), p. 628. Perry's grim portrait of Puritan morality can be used to describe similar aspects of Humanist thought. In this connection see Spitz, *Patterns of Anti-Democratic Thought*, pp. 271–72.

42. More's statement on the elusiveness of the inner check is quoted in Trilling, *Matthew Arnold*, p. 343; More, *Aristocracy and Justice*, pp. 30, 136, 141. For Nock's analysis of these matters, see a more detailed discussion of *Our Enemy, the State* in Chapter 7.

43. Babbitt, *Democracy and Leadership*, p. 296; Kazin, *On Native Grounds*, p. 309.

44. Foerster, ed., Preface to *Humanism and America*, p. xiii; Babbitt, *Democracy and Leadership*, pp. 251–52, 244–47, 307.

45. Babbitt, *Democracy and Leadership*, p. 246; Allen Tate, "The Fallacy of Humanism," in *Critique of Humanism*, p. 132; Kazin, *On Native Grounds*, pp. 293, 309–11; Stuart Sherman, *The Main Stream*, p. 31; Seward Collins, "A Witness for the Government," *American Review* 6 (Nov. 1935):106–11; Babbitt, *Democracy and Leadership*, pp. 77, 127, 147–49, 170, 302. For a study of the tendency of Humanism to support fascism, see John R. Harrison, *The Reactionaries, Yeats, Lewis, Pound, Eliot, Lawrence: A Study of the Anti-Democratic Intelligentsia* (New York, 1967).

46. More on Thoreau as quoted in Kazin, *On Native Grounds*, p. 309; Babbitt, *Democracy and Leadership*, p. 261.

47. Nock, "Anarchist's Progress," *On Doing*, pp. 157, 152.

48. Nock, "Cultural Forecast," p. 94.

49. For this interpretation of Emerson's "American Scholar," see George M. Fredrickson, *The Inner Civil War: Northern Intellectuals and the Crisis of the Union* (New York, 1965), pp. 10–12.

50. Nock to Mrs. Evans, 6 Feb. 1926, *Letters*, p. 22.

51. Emerson quoted in George Woodcock, *Anarchism*, p. 454; Henry David Thoreau, "Civil Disobedience," in Staughton Lynd, ed., *Nonviolence in America: A Documentary History* (New York, 1966), p. 61; Nock, the title essay in *On Doing*, pp. 170–73.

52. Benj[amin] Tucker, *Instead of a Book*, p. 15; Nock, "On Doing the Right Thing," p. 174, and see pp. 175, 177–78.

53. Nock, "On Doing," pp. 175, 177, 178.

54. For recent criticism of the managed society that reflects the earlier concerns of Nock, see Paul Goodman, *Growing Up Absurd* (New York, 1960), Theodore Roszak, *The Making of a Counter Culture* (New York, 1969); and Charles Reich, *The Greening of America* (New York, 1970). While the solutions these authors present may be very different from what Nock would have endorsed, their critical analysis of existing society is often strikingly similar.

55. George Woodcock, *Anarchism*, p. 469; David Riesman, Nathan Glazer, and Reuel Denney, *The Lonely Crowd: A Study of the Changing American Character* (New Haven, 1950), passim; C. Wright Mills, *White Collar: The American Middle Classes* (New York, 1953), p. xii; Walt Whitman, "Democratic Vistas," in Mark Van Doren, ed., *The Portable Walt*

Whitman (New York, 1945), pp. 407, 430; Dwight Macdonald, *Against the American Grain* (New York, 1962), p. 72.

56. Woodcock, *Anarchism*, p. 470. See also Judith Shklar, "Political Theory of Utopia," *Daedalus* 94 (spring 1965):370, 378, for a discussion of the tension between the longing for utopia and the nostalgia for antiquity that has characterized dissenters.

57. Nock to Mrs. Evans, 29 Sept. 1929, *Letters*, p. 40. See also Nock, *A Journey into Rabelais's France*, p. 89.

58. Nock and C. R. Wilson, *Francis Rabelais: The Man and His Work*; Nock and Wilson, eds., *The Works of Francis Rabelais*.

59. Van Wyck Brooks, *Days of the Phoenix*, p. 59. See also Nock to Mrs. Evans, 29 Sept. 1929, *Letters*, p. 40.

60. Nock, "Pantagruelism," *Analysis* 2 (Aug. 1946):6. *Analysis* was a libertarian periodical edited by Frank Chodorov. Its masthead carried a quotation from Victor Cousin: "Only individuals exist, and in the individual, nothing but the individual." Nock's address to the medical faculty of Johns Hopkins was delivered on 28 October 1932. Copies of *Analysis* were given to me by Robert Crunden.

61. Nock, *Rabelais: The Man and His Work*, p. 358; Anatole France, *Rabelais*, trans. Ernest Boyd (London, 1925), p. 276.

62. Nock, *Rabelais*, pp. 127, 326; *Journey into Rabelais's France*, p. 47.

63. Nock, "Pantagruelism," p. 6; Nock to Mrs. Evans, 29 Sept. 1929, *Letters*, p. 40.

64. Nock, *Rabelais*, p. 327; see also pp. 326, 328; Nock, *Journey into Rabelais's France*, p. 47.

65. Sir Thomas Urquhart and Peter Motteux, *The Complete Works of Doctor François Rabelais*, vol. 1 (New York, 1927), bk. 1, chaps. 27, 52, 57, pp. 111, 197, 213–14.

66. Nock, *Rabelais*, pp. 195–96.

67. Urquhart and Motteux, *Works of Rabelais*, vol. 1, chaps. 52, 57, 54, pp. 198–99, 214, 203–4; Nock, *Rabelais*, p. 194.

68. Nock, *Rabelais*, pp. 358–59.

69. Nock, "Pantagruelism," p. 6.

6. The Revelation of Cram

1. W. C. Bullitt, *It's Not Done* (New York, 1926), p. 371.
2. Lippmann quoted in Arthur M. Schlesinger, Jr., *The Age of Roosevelt,*

vol. 1, *The Crisis of the Old Order, 1919–1933* (Cambridge, Mass., 1957), p. 151.

3. Lawrence Cremin, *The Transformation of the School: Progressivism in American Education* (New York, 1961), p. lx.

4. Abraham Flexner, *Universities: American, English, and German* (1967), pp. 103, 133, 144, 153–56.

5. Nock to Edmund C. Evans, 6 Nov. 1930, *Letters*, p. 46; Ellery Sedgwick to Nock, 26 Feb. 1930, transcript of letter in Crunden Papers.

6. Nock to Evans, 1930, *Letters*, p. 43.

7. Flexner, *Universities*, p. 4.

8. Nock, *Theory of Education in the United States*, pp. 30, 38–39. And p. 34.

9. Nock, "Thoughts from Abroad," *Free Speech and Plain Language*, p. 108. See also Nock, *Theory of Education*, pp. 42–46, and "Thoughts," pp. 107, 109.

10. Nock, "Thoughts," p. 108; *Theory of Education*, pp. 42–43; "Thoughts," pp. 108–9; Godkin quoted in Alan P. Grimes, *American Political Thought* (New York, 1955), p. 397.

11. Nock, *Theory of Education*, p. 55.

12. Ibid., pp. 114, 140. And pp. 113, 135, 138–39.

13. Arthur Bestor, *The Restoration of Learning*, pp. 113–16.

14. Nock, *Theory of Education*, pp. 58–59; Richard Hofstadter, *Anti-Intellectualism in American Life* (1966), pp. 344, 355–56.

15. Merle Curti, *The Social Ideas of American Educators* (New York, 1935), pp. 486–87.

16. Nock, *Theory of Education*, p. 121. And pp. 79–80, 116, 125–27.

17. Ibid., pp. 94–106, 151–54, 159–60.

18. Paul Goodman, *Compulsory Mis-education and The Community of Scholars* (New York, Vintage Books, 1964), pp. 113, 134.

19. Nock, *Journal of Forgotten Days*, 26 Aug. 1935, pp. 104, 105. This intimate journal was edited by Nock's sons and published after his death.

20. Ralph Adams Cram, *My Life in Architecture*, pp. 57, 97, 224–28.

21. Ibid., pp. 50–57, 97, 224, 136, 260.

22. Cram, *The Nemesis of Mediocrity*, pp. 22–23, 5. And p. 33.

23. Ibid., pp. 46, 50.

24. Cram, *Nemesis of Mediocrity*, p. 35; John Higham, *Strangers in the Land: Patterns of American Nativism* (New York, 1963), pp. 102–3.

25. Cram, *Nemesis of Mediocrity*, pp. 37, 40, 41; Grant quoted in Higham, *Strangers in the Land*, p. 156. And Cram, op. cit., p. 38.

26. Cram, "Why We Do Not Behave Like Human Beings," *American Mercury* 27 (Sept. 1932):41–48.

27. Ibid., p. 48.

28. See Nock, *Journal of These Days*, 10 Sept. 1932, pp. 43–44.

29. Michael Harrington, *The Accidental Century* (Baltimore, 1965), p. 209.

30. Samuel David McConnell, *Immortability: An Old Man's Conclusions* (New York, 1930), pp. 20–21, 45–55, 104–5.

31. José Ortega y Gasset, *The Revolt of the Masses* (New York, 1932), pp. 1, 7, 63, 88 (page references are to the New American Library Mentor Book edition [New York, 1952]).

32. Nock, "Are All Men Human?" *Harper's Magazine* 166 (Jan. 1933):241, 242.

33. Ibid., p. 243.

34. Ibid., p. 244.

35. Nock, "The Quest of the Missing Link," *Atlantic Monthly* 155 (Apr. 1935):399–408.

36. Ibid., p. 401.

37. Ibid., p. 402; *Journal of These Days*, 16 Feb. 1933, pp. 127–28.

38. Nock, "Quest of the Missing Link," p. 403.

39. Nock, "The Gods' Lookout," *Free Speech*, pp. 305–25; this essay was written in February 1934.

40. Nock, *Free Speech*, p. 322; *Memoirs* (1964), pp. 132, 133.

41. Nock, "Quest of the Missing Link," pp. 405, 406.

42. Ibid., p. 406; Lionel Trilling, *Matthew Arnold* (1949), pp. 269–70.

43. Nock to Paul Palmer, 13 Mar. 1943, Palmer Papers; Nock, *Memoirs*, p. 138; see also pp. 136–37, 139, 140, 303, 310–13. In a letter to Ruth Robinson, 4 Oct. 1946, Nock's son Francis wrote of the important influence of Cram, which challenged his father's faith in the possibility of an "enlightened anarchy" (Robinson Papers).

44. *Memoirs*, p. 138; Arthur Schopenhauer, "Further Psychological Observations," *Studies in Pessimism: A Series of Essays*, trans. Thomas Bailey Saunders (London, 1913), p. 62.

7. Anarchist Attentats

1. Nock, *Journal of These Days*, 16 Apr. 1933, 7 Oct. 1932, pp. 161, 56.

2. Ibid., 11 May 1933, p. 180.

3. Nock, "Impostor-Terms," *Free Speech and Plain Language,* p. 294. See also pp. 292–93, 295; and Nock, *Our Enemy, the State,* pp. 188–200.

4. Nock, *Journal of These Days,* 8 Nov. 1932, pp. 73–74. And 10 Oct. 1932, pp. 57–58.

5. Ibid., 10 Nov. 1932, p. 74. And 25 Feb. 1933, p. 133.

6. Nock to Edmund C. Evans, 16 Sept. 1933, *Letters,* p. 56. And *Journal of These Days,* 11 May 1933, p. 179.

7. Nock, *Journal of These Days,* 16 Dec. 1933, 30 Oct. 1933, pp. 296, 261. And *Journal of Forgotten Days,* 20 June 1934, p. 23; *Journal of These Days,* 8 Nov. 1933, p. 268.

8. Nock, *Journal of These Days,* 16 Sept. 1932, p. 47.

9. Nock, *Journal of Forgotten Days,* 24 Aug. 1934, p. 44.

10. Ibid., 21 July 1934, pp. 30–31.

11. Nock to Mrs. Evans, June 1935, *Letters,* p. 72 n.; *Journal of These Days,* 29 Nov. 1933, p. 280. And Nock to Bernard Iddings Bell, January 1934[?], *Selected Letters,* pp. 114–15.

12. Nock, *Our Enemy,* pp. 36–38, 49–50.

13. Quoted in Adrienne Koch and William Peden, eds., *The Life and Selected Writings of Thomas Jefferson* (New York, 1944), pp. 221–22; Nock, *Our Enemy,* pp. 36–39.

14. Enrico Malatesta, "Anarchism and Government," in Irving L. Horowitz, ed., *The Anarchists,* p. 74; Randolph Bourne, "The State," *War and the Intellectuals,* pp. 67–69.

15. Nock, *Our Enemy,* p. 97; see also pp. 58–62, 68–71, 93–94, 96, 98.

16. Ibid., p. 159. And pp. 91–92, 144–45, 152–57, 168–69.

17. Ibid., pp. 9–10, 57.

18. Ibid., pp. 148–49, 52 n.

19. Ibid., p. 5. See also Nock to Evans, 25 Oct. 1933, *Letters,* pp. 58–59.

20. Nock, *Our Enemy,* pp. 3, 6, 151–52; see also pp. 4–5, 52–57, 148–50, 204–5.

21. George Soule, "Presenting the Case for Individualism," *Saturday Review of Literature* 13 (11 Jan. 1936):6; Seward Collins, "A Witness for the Government," *American Review* 6 (Nov. 1935):106–11.

22. Nock, *Our Enemy,* p. 11.

23. Richard Hofstadter, *The Paranoid Style in American Politics and Other Essays* (New York, Vintage Books, 1965), chap. 1; Nock, *Journal of Forgotten Days,* 27 Sept. 1934, p. 59; Nock, *Memoirs* (1964), p. 126; Eric Goldman, "Aristocratic Dogma," *New York Times Book Review,* 29 Nov. 1964, p. 14.

24. Nock, *Our Enemy*, p. 187 n.

25. R. H. S. Crossman, *The Politics of Socialism* (New York, 1965), p. 57; Hans Morganthau, "What Ails America," *New Republic* 157 (28 Oct. 1967):17.

26. Compare, e.g., Nock's arguments in *Our Enemy*, pp. 87–89, with the thesis of Gabriel Kolko in *The Triumph of Conservatism: A Reinterpretation of American History* (Glencoe, Ill., 1963), passim.

27. Nock, *Our Enemy*, pp. 26, 27. And pp. 28–31; *Journal of These Days*, 26 Dec. 1932, pp. 101–2.

28. Crunden, *Mind and Art of Nock*, p. 157. On p. 158 Crunden concedes that Nock "hoped only that some of his Remnant might happen upon the book." There is a real contradiction here since "men of action" were hardly a part of Nock's Remnant. See Nock's statement on the practical futility of the book, *Our Enemy*, pp. 206–7; Nock, *Journal of Forgotten Days*, 23 Jan. 1935, p. 94; Richard Hofstadter, *The Paranoid Style*, p. 38.

29. Nock, "Isaiah's Job," *Atlantic Monthly* 157 (June 1936):641–49. This essay is reprinted in *Free Speech*, pp. 248–65.

30. Ralph Hayes to Newton D. Baker, 17 June 1936, Newton Baker Manuscript Collection, Box 117, Library of Congress. I am grateful to Professor William Leuchtenburg for drawing my attention to this letter.

31. Nock, "Isaiah's Job," p. 259; *Journal of These Days*, 13 Sept. 1933, p. 248.

32. Nock, *Journal of Forgotten Days*, 31 July 1934, p. 33; Nock to Mrs. Evans, Nov. 1937, *Letters*, p. 95.

33. Digby Baltzell, *The Protestant Establishment*, pp. 248–49.

34. Nock, *Journal of These Days*, 19 Nov. 1932, 30 Mar. 1933, 28 Sept. 1933, 18 Dec. 1933, pp. 84, 150, 256, 298.

35. Nock, *Journal of Forgotten Days*, 6 June 1934, 31 Aug. 1934, 12 Aug. 1934, pp. 17, 47, 40.

36. Nock, "The Jewish Problem in America," *Atlantic Monthly* 167 (June 1941):699–706.

37. Nock, "The Jewish Problem in America," *Atlantic Monthly* 168 (July 1941):68–76; Edna Ferber, Letter to the editor, "Atlantic Repartee," *Atlantic Monthly* 168 (Sept. 1941).

38. Nock to Paul Palmer, 13 Dec. 1943, Palmer Papers.

39. Nock, *Journal of Forgotten Days*, 30 May 1934, p. 13. And Barbara M. Solomon, *Ancestors and Immigrants*, p. 40. In addition to the source material in Worthington C. Ford, ed., *Letters of Henry Adams*, 2 vols. (Boston, 1938); and Henry Adams, *The Education of Henry Adams* (Boston, 1918), I

have relied heavily on the interpretations of Solomon, *Ancestors and Immigrants;* Allen Guttmann, *The Conservative Tradition in America;* and Frederic Cople Jaher, *Doubters and Dissenters.*

40. Henry Adams, *Education of Henry Adams,* p. 238; Nock, *Memoirs,* p. 178; *Journal of Forgotten Days,* p. 13. On the view that for Adams anti-Semitism transcended a symbolic protest against capitalism, see Solomon, *Ancestors and Immigrants,* p. 41.

41. Adams cited in Solomon, *Ancestors and Immigrants,* p. 34, and Guttmann, *Conservative Tradition,* pp. 135, 134. Both Solomon and Guttmann stress Adams's early identification and sympathy with what he felt was a radical democratic ideology.

42. Nock, "The Disadvantages of Being Educated," *Harper's Magazine* 165 (Sept. 1932):500; Adams to Elizabeth Cameron, 15 Feb. 1914, *Letters of Henry Adams,* 2:622; Nock to Paul Palmer, 13 Dec. 1943, Palmer Papers; Solomon, *Ancestors and Immigrants,* p. 42.

43. Ralph Adams Cram, "Why We Do Not Behave Like Human Beings," *American Mercury* 44 (Aug. 1938):418–28.

44. Nock, "The State of the Union: No More Rabbits in the Hat," *American Mercury* 44 (July 1938):334; and "State of the Union: Postscript on the Royal Visit," *American Mercury* 48 (Sept. 1939):102–5; Paul Palmer to Nock, 27 Dec., 5 Aug., and 30 Sept. 1938, Palmer Papers.

45. Nock, "You Can't Do Business with Hitler," *Scribner's Commentator* 11 (Nov. 1941):84–85. For the activities and character of *Scribner's Commentator,* see John Roy Carlson, *Undercover* (New York, 1943), pp. 203, 207, 247, 256; and *The Plotters* (New York, 1946), pp. 112–13, 203; *New York Times,* 6 Nov. 1941, p. 11; *Time* 36 (30 Dec. 1940):34.

46. Carlson, *The Plotters,* pp. 23, 281–84; Ralph Lord Roy, *Apostles of Discord: A Study of Organized Bigotry* (Boston, 1953), p. 234; Wayne Cole, *America First* (Madison, Wis., 1953), pp. 73, 118–19.

47. Nock to Mrs. Evans and Miss Winsor, 21 Sept. 1944, *Letters,* pp. 205–6.

48. Nock, *Henry George: An Essay,* pp. 7, 153. And p. 8.

49. Ibid., p. 220. And pp. 118–20.

50. Nock, *Memoirs,* p. 149. In a letter, 26 Oct. 1913, to Ruth Robinson, Nock complained that his articles sounded as though they had been "written from a seat in the grand stand" and hoped he could become more involved (Robinson Papers).

51. *Memoirs,* p. 99.

52. Ernest Sutherland Bates, "About Half of Henry George," *New York Herald Tribune, Books,* 27 Aug. 1939, p. 5.

Epilogue

1. Nock to Paul Palmer, 7 July 1942, 13 Dec. 1943, Palmer Papers.

2. Lincoln Colcord to Nock, 3 Apr. 1944, Nock Papers; Villard to Nock, Nov. 1944, Villard Papers; Dorothy Thompson to Villard, 12 Nov. 1945, Villard Papers; Charles Beard to Villard, 20 Oct. 1944, Villard Papers.

3. Nock to Miss Winsor, 11 Oct. 1943, Nock to Mrs. Evans and Miss Winsor, 23 Nov. 1943, *Letters*, pp. 188–90; Nock to Felix M. Oliva, 16 May 1944, *Selected Letters*, p. 161.

4. Merrill Peterson, Introduction to Nock, *Jefferson* (1960), p. vii; Joe Flaherty, "Up the Up Staircase: Educating the Plebes," *Village Voice*, 18 Jan. 1968, p. 5.

5. Leonard E. Read, *Activities at FEE*, n.d., and *Notes from FEE*, July 1962, Foundation for Economic Education, Inc., Irvington-on-Hudson, N.Y.

6. Murray N. Rothbard, "The General Line," *Left and Right* 1 (spring 1965):3; Carl Oglesby and Richard Shaull, *Containment and Change* (New York, 1967), p. 167.

7. James Reston, "Washington: The President Decides," *New York Times*, 2 Feb. 1966, p. 46; Daniel Moynihan, *New York Times*, 24 Sept. 1968, p. 1; William Appleman Williams, "Williams on Policy for U.S. Radicals," *National Guardian*, 27 Nov. 1965, p. 7; Oglesby, *Containment and Change*, p. 167.

8. Nock, "Our Elderly Young," *The Book of Journeyman*, pp. 37, 38.

9. Herbert Marcuse, *One-Dimensional Man* (Boston, 1966), pp. 4–9 and passim.

10. Andrew Hacker, "Philosopher on the New Left," *New York Times Book Review*, 10 Mar. 1968, p. 34; Michael Harrington, "The Mystical Militants," *New Republic* 154 (19 Feb. 1966):22.

Bibliography

Primary Sources

MANUSCRIPTS

Bolton-Hall Papers   Bolton-Hall Papers. Manuscript Division. New York Public Library.
A few letters by Nock concerning liberal causes in the twenties.

Crunden Papers   Robert M. Crunden Papers. Albert Jay Nock Collection. Historical Manuscript Division. Yale University Library.
Letters and duplicated material gathered by Crunden in preparing his study of Nock; particularly useful for various judgments of Nock by his associates.

Huebsch *Freeman*   B. W. Huebsch annotated edition of the *Freeman*. Manuscript Division. Butler Library. Columbia University.
Indispensable for determining authorship of unsigned articles and editorials.

Huebsch Papers   Benjamin W. Huebsch Papers. Manuscript Division. Library of Congress.
Interesting material on the *Freeman*.

Nagel Papers   Charles Nagel Papers. Historical Manuscript Division. Yale University Library.
About twenty Nock letters written, for the most part, when he was editor of the *Freeman*.

Nock Papers   Albert J. Nock Papers. Manuscript Division. Library of Congress.

A fairly extensive collection of correspondence and Nock manuscripts; of particular interest is Nock's correspondence, during the last years of his life, with Lincoln Colcord (folders AC-9150 in a box labeled *"Manuscript of Our Enemy the State"*).

Palmer Papers Paul Palmer Papers. Albert Jay Nock Collection. Historical Manuscript Division. Yale University Library. Correspondence and miscellaneous material deposited by Nock's friend, who was editor of the *American Mercury* in the late thirties; contains many Nock letters, as well as interesting letters from Ralph Adams Cram and other friends and associates.

Robinson Papers Ruth Robinson Papers. Albert Jay Nock Collection. Historical Manuscript Division. Yale University Library.
Only recently opened to scholars; six volumes of Nock letters, in typescript, to Miss Robinson, written from 1912 until his death; an important autobiographical sketch; notes made by Miss Robinson; letters from Nock's two sons and friends after his death; an extensive clipping collection; and memorabilia.

Spingarn Collection Joel E. Springarn Collection. Manuscript Division. New York Public Library.
Approximately six letters from Nock written in the early twenties.

Villard Papers Oswald Garrison Villard Papers. Houghton Library. Harvard University.
Extensive Nock-Villard correspondence concerning Nock's work on the *Nation* and the *Freeman,* as well as political and social comment throughout the period of Nock's professional career.

Whitlock Papers Brand Whitlock Papers. Manuscript Division. Library of Congress.
Robert Crunden has informed me that there are about two dozen Nock letters deceptively filed in this collection, but I have not seen them.

BOOKS BY NOCK

The Book of Journeyman: Essays from the "New Freeman." New York: Publishers of the *New Freeman*, 1930.

Francis Rabelais: The Man and His Work. With C. R. Wilson. New York: Harper & Brothers, 1929.

Free Speech and Plain Language. New York: William Morrow & Co., 1937.

Henry George: An Essay. New York: William Morrow & Co., 1939.

Jefferson. New York: Harcourt, Brace & Co., 1926. New York: Hill & Wang, 1960.

Journal of Forgotten Days: May 1934–October 1935. Hinsdale, Ill.: Henry Regnery Co., 1948.

A Journal of These Days: June 1932–December 1933. New York: William Morrow & Co., 1934.

A Journey into Rabelais's France. New York: William Morrow & Co., 1934.

Letters from Albert Jay Nock, 1924–1945, to Edmund C. Evans, Mrs. Edmund C. Evans, and Ellen Winsor. [Edited by Frank W. Garrison.] Caldwell, Ida.: Caxton Printers, 1949.

Memoirs of a Superfluous Man. New York: Harper & Brothers, 1943. Chicago: Henry Regnery Co., 1964.

The Myth of a Guilty Nation. New York: B. W. Huebsch, 1922.

On Doing the Right Thing and Other Essays. New York: Harper & Brothers, 1928.

Our Enemy, the State. New York: William Morrow & Co., 1935.

Selected Letters of Albert Jay Nock. Edited by Francis J. Nock. Caldwell, Ida.: Caxton Printers, 1962.

Snoring as a Fine Art and Twelve Other Essays. Rindge, N.H.: Richard R. Smith, 1958.

The Theory of Education in the United States. New York: Harcourt, Brace & Co., 1932.

The Works of Francis Rabelais. Edited with Catherine Rose Wilson. New York: Harcourt, Brace & Co., 1931.

INTRODUCTIONS BY NOCK

The "Freeman" Book: Typical Editorials, Essays, Critiques, and Other Selections from the Eight Volumes of the "Freeman," 1920–1924. New York: B. W. Huebsch, 1924.

[HASKINS, HENRY STANLEY.] *Meditations in Wall Street.* New York: William Morrow & Co., 1940.

[NEILSON, FRANCIS.] *How Diplomats Make War.* New York: B. W. Huebsch, 1915, 1916.

NOCK, ALBERT JAY, ed. *Selected Works of Artemus Ward.* New York: Albert and Charles Boni, 1924.

SPENCER, HERBERT. *The Man versus the State.* Caldwell, Ida.: Caxton Printers, 1940.

WHITLOCK, BRAND. *Forty Years of It.* New York: D. Appleton & Co., 1914.

Secondary Sources

This is a selective list of books and articles dealing with, or related to, Nock's life and work. For a more extensive list see Crunden and Cziraky. Other references are in the notes.

BAKER, RAY STANNARD. *American Chronicle.* New York: Charles Scribner's Sons, 1945.
Useful for material on the *American Magazine.*

BALTZELL, E. DIGBY. *The Protestant Establishment: Aristocracy and Caste in America.* New York: Random House, Vintage Books, 1964.
Has a chapter on the Establishment reaction to President Franklin D. Roosevelt.

BELL, BERNARD IDDINGS. *Crowd Culture.* New York: Harper & Brothers, 1952. Chicago: Henry Regnery Co., 1956.
A criticism of mass culture by a close friend of Nock.

———. "The Virginia Lectures on Education." *Analysis* 2 (Aug. 1946):2.
An analysis of Nock's Page-Barbour Lectures.

BESTOR, ARTHUR. *The Restoration of Learning: A Program for Redeeming the Unfulfilled Promise of American Education.* New York: Alfred A. Knopf, 1955.
A devastating criticism of professional educators; supports many of Nock's arguments.

BOURNE, RANDOLPH S. *War and the Intellectuals: Essays, 1915–1919.* Edited by Carl Resek. New York: Harper & Row, 1964.
A brilliant critique of the intellectuals' complicity with the war machine, these essays parallel much of Nock's thought during World War I.

———. *The World of Randolph Bourne.* Edited by Lillian Schlissel. New York: E. P. Dutton & Co., 1965.
A comprehensive collection of Bourne's writings with a good selection of his letters; reveals the quality of cultural dissent during the progressive era and World War I.

BROOKS, VAN WYCK. *Days of the Phoenix: The Nineteen-Twenties I Remember.* New York: E. P. Dutton & Co., 1957.
Contains an interesting analysis of the *Freeman* editorial staff, with particular attention to Nock.

CHODOROV, FRANK. "The Articulate Individualist." *Analysis* 2 (Aug. 1946):1–2.
A strong libertarian anarchist's appreciation of Nock.

———. "Gentle Nock at Our Door." *Fragments* 4 (Apr.–June, 1966):2.
A brief, sympathetic survey of Nock's ideas.

COLCORD, LINCOLN. "A Superfluous Man?" *Analysis* 2 (Aug. 1946):8.
Almost a review of Nock's *Memoirs;* shows that Nock's proposals could be applied, even after his death, to the problems of society.

CRAM, RALPH ADAMS. *Convictions and Controversies.* Boston: Marshall Jones Co., 1935.
A collection of Cram's contentious essays.

———. *My Life in Architecture.* Boston: Little, Brown & Co., 1936.
A vigorous autobiographical account of Cram's work and ideas.

———. *The Nemesis of Mediocrity.* Boston: Marshall Jones Co., 1917.
An explicit statement of Cram's racist and elitist views.

CRUNDEN, ROBERT M. *The Mind and Art of Albert Jay Nock.* Chicago: Henry Regnery Co., 1964.
Written as an undergraduate honors thesis at Yale University under the direction of Professor Edmund S. Morgan; an able, sympathetic exposition of Nock's philosophy.

CZIRAKY, J. SANDOR. *The Evolution of the Social Philosophy of Albert Jay Nock.* Ann Arbor, Mich.: University Microfilms, 1959.
An uncritical chronological account of Nock's life and work; useful bibliography.

DRINNON, RICHARD. *Rebel in Paradise: A Biography of Emma Goldman.* Chicago: University of Chicago Press, 1961.
A fascinating account of a flamboyant anarchist; particularly useful in explaining the bridge between European and native American radicalism.

FLEXNER, ABRAHAM. *Universities: American, English, and German.* New York: Oxford University Press, 1930. New York: Teachers College Press, 1967.
A scathing attack on the puerilities of some of America's most prestigious institutions of higher education; certainly an inspiration for Nock's lectures on education.

FORCEY, CHARLES. *The Crossroads of Liberalism: Croly, Weyl, Lippmann, and the Progressive Era, 1900–1925.* New York: Oxford University Press, 1961.
The best account of the dilemmas of liberalism during the period.

GRAHAM, OTIS L. *An Encore for Reform: The Old Progressives and the New Deal.* New York: Oxford University Press, 1967.
An interesting biographical analysis of what happened to the progressives when confronted with the New Deal.

GUTTMANN, ALLEN. *The Conservative Tradition in America.* New York: Oxford University Press, 1967.
An important analysis of conservative thought, which he sees as enduring primarily in the literary and religious imagination.

HOFFMAN, FREDERICK J. *The Twenties: American Writing in the Postwar Decade.* New York: Viking Press, 1955.
An extensive critical study of literary trends in the twenties; particularly useful on the Humanist controversy.

HOFSTADTER, RICHARD. *Anti-Intellectualism in American Life.* New
York: Alfred A. Knopf, 1963. New York: Random House, Vintage
Books, 1966.
A particularly useful analysis of John Dewey and the development of
progressive education.

———. *The Paranoid Style in American Politics.* New York: Alfred A.
Knopf, 1965.
An acute analysis of the mental machinations of political extremism;
useful for trying to understand some of Nock's eccentric attitudes.

HOROWITZ, IRVING L., ed. *The Anarchists.* New York: Dell Publishing Co.,
1964.
An anthology of European and American anarchist writings, with a
comprehensive introduction and concluding summary.

JAHER, FREDERIC COPLE. *Doubters and Dissenters: Cataclysmic Thought in
America, 1885–1918.* New York: Free Press of Glencoe, 1964.
A good study of the alienated at the turn of the century; particularly
useful for the analysis of Henry Adams's despair.

JOLL, JAMES. *The Anarchists.* Boston: Little, Brown & Co., 1964.
A beautifully written history of anarchism, concerned primarily with
its development in Europe.

KLEINFELD, LEONARD F. "Nock Lauds Thoreau." *Fragments* 4 (Apr.–June
1966):9.
An interesting development of Nock's appreciation of Thoreau.

KRIMERMAN, LEONARD I., and PERRY, LEWIS, eds. *Patterns of Anarchy.* New
York: Doubleday & Co., Anchor Books, 1966.
An extensive topical anthology of anarchist writers; especially useful
for tracing some of Nock's ideas.

LASCH, CHRISTOPHER. *The New Radicalism in America, 1889–1963: The Intellectual as a Social Type.* New York: Alfred A. Knopf, 1965.
A provocative study of a group of offbeat progressive thinkers in this
century; particularly useful for the progressive period; helps place
Nock in his intellectual milieu.

MACLENNAN, HUGH. "Speaking of Books." *New York Times Book Review,*
30 Sept. 1962, p. 2.
Places Nock in the aristocratic elitist tradition in America.

Bibliography

MCLOUGHLIN, WILLIAM G. "Pietism and the American Character." *American Quarterly* 17 (summer 1965):165 ff.
Persuasively challenges the concepts of pragmatism and democratic liberalism as a key to the American character and offers the pietistic temper as an alternative; the discussion of the conflict between those who seek perfect moral order and those who seek perfect moral freedom is particularly useful for understanding Nock's anarchism.

MARTIN, JAMES J. *Men against the State: The Expositors of Individualist Anarchism in America, 1827–1908.* De Kalb, Ill.: Adrian Allen Associates, 1953.
A useful historical survey of American anarchism.

NEILSON, FRANCIS. *My Life in Two Worlds.* Appleton, Wis.: C. C. Nelson Publishing Co., 1952.
Valuable for material about Nock's career on the *Nation* and the *Freeman* and particularly for the source of some of his economic ideas.

———. "The Story of *The Freeman*." *American Journal of Economics and Sociology,* vol. 6, supplement (Oct. 1946).
A cantankerous attack on Nock's intellectual integrity, suggesting that he was a dilettante and plagiarizer of ideas; despite its unfortunate tone it contains interesting information about the editorial policy of the *Freeman*.

OPITZ, EDMUND A. "Man of Culture." *Fragments* 4 (Apr.–June, 1966):1.
An admirer's sympathetic estimate of Nock's role as a spokesman for the saving Remnant.

OPPENHEIMER, FRANZ. *The State: Its History and Development Viewed Sociologically.* Translated by John M. Gitterman. Indianapolis: Bobbs-Merrill Co., 1914.
The work that most influenced Nock's criticism of the state.

ROSENFELD, PAUL. *Men Seen.* New York: Dial Press, 1925.
A vigorous criticism of Nock's aesthetic judgments as editor of the *Freeman*.

ROSSITER, CLINTON LAWRENCE. *Conservatism in America: The Thankless Persuasion.* New York: Alfred A. Knopf, 1955. 2d ed., rev. New York: Random House, Vintage Books, 1962.

A comprehensive survey of conservative thought that places Nock
and other anarchists in the conservative fold.

ROTHBARD, MURRAY N. "Albert Jay Nock, Radical." *Fragments* (Apr.–June
1966):8.
An article by a laissez-faire economist who insists on the radicalism
of Nock's individualism.

SCHUSTER, EUNICE MINETTE. *Native American Anarchism: A Study of Left-
Wing American Individualism.* Smith College Studies in History, vol.
17. Northampton, Mass.: Smith College, Oct. 1931–July 1932.
The standard study of American anarchism; has an interesting
discussion of the relationship between anarchists and single-taxers.

SEDGWICK, ELLERY. *The Happy Profession.* Boston: Little, Brown & Co.,
1946.
The memoirs of Nock's editor on the *Atlantic Monthly*, with an
informed appreciation of Nock.

SHERMAN, STUART. *The Main Stream.* New York: Charles Scribner's Sons,
1927.
Contains a perceptive review of Nock's *Jefferson* and recognition of
Nock's anarchistic perfectionism.

SOLOMON, BARBARA MILLER. *Ancestors and Immigrants: A Changing New
England Tradition.* Cambridge: Harvard University Press, 1956.
An excellent analysis of the sources of anti-Semitism in Henry
Adams and other Brahmins.

STEARNS, HAROLD E., ed. *Civilization in the United States, an Inquiry by
Thirty Americans.* New York: Harcourt, Brace & Co., 1922.
A polemical appraisal of the state of American culture at the start of
the twenties; contains George Soule's skeptical analysis of the *Freeman*'s radicalism.

SYMES, LILLIAN, and CLEMENT, TRAVERS. *Rebel America: The Story of Social
Revolt in the United States.* New York: Harper & Brothers, 1934.
A radical history of American protest with some interesting remarks
on the *Freeman*'s position in relation to other dissenting magazines.

THORNTON, ROBERT MONROE. "Albert Jay Nock: An Appreciation." Mimeo-
graphed. New York: The Nockian Society, 1964.

A good example of the almost religious devotion of a contemporary "acolyte" and member of the Nockian Society; the pamphlet has been updated in a paperback edition, *Cogitations from Albert Jay Nock* (Irvington-on-Hudson, N.Y.: The Nockian Society, 1970).

————, ed. *The Wisdom of Albert Jay Nock: A Collection of Quotations.* Irvington-on-Hudson, N.Y.: The Nockian Society, 1965.
An attractive selection.

TRILLING, LIONEL. *Matthew Arnold.* London: George Allen & Unwin, 1939. New York: Columbia University Press, 1949.
A definitive and beautifully written critical analysis of Arnold; particularly useful in understanding Nock's ideas concerning the saving Remnant.

TUCKER, BENJ[AMIN] R. *Instead of a Book, by a Man Too Busy to Write One: A Fragmentary Exposition of Philosophical Anarchism.* New York: B. R. Tucker, 1897.
A vast collection of Tucker's writings from his anarchist magazine *Liberty*; particularly useful for the anarchist debates with other radicals.

TURNER, SUSAN J. *A History of the "Freeman": Literary Landmark of the Early Twenties.* New York: Columbia University Press, 1963.
A scholarly study of the *Freeman*, full of interesting material about members of the staff, and with an analysis of the magazine's literary, artistic, and political position.

WOODCOCK, GEORGE. *Anarchism: A History of Libertarian Ideas and Movements.* New York: World Publishing Co., Meridian Books, 1962.
One of the best surveys of anarchist thought.

WRESZIN, MICHAEL. *Oswald Garrison Villard: Pacifist at War.* Bloomington, Ind.: Indiana University Press, 1965.
Helpful as a study of the liberal mentality against which Nock revolted

Index

Index

Index

Index

Index

DATE DUE
